P9-DMU-961

How to Make a Massachusetts Will

With Forms

Joseph P. DiBlasi
Mark Warda
Attorneys at Law

SPHINX PUBLISHING
Sphinx International, Inc.
1725 Clearwater-Largo Rd., S.
Post Office Box 25
Clearwater, FL 34617
Tel. (813) 587-0999
Fax (813) 586-5088

SPHINX®
is a registered trademark of Sphinx International, Inc.

> Note: The law changes constantly and is subject to different interpretations. It is up to you to check it thoroughly before relying on it. Neither the author nor the publisher guarantees the outcome of the uses to which this material is put.

This publication is designed to provide accurate and authoritative information in regard to the subject matter covered. It is sold with the understanding that the publisher is not engaged in rendering legal, accounting or other professional services. If legal advice or other expert assistance is required, the service of a competent professional person should be sought.

- From a Declaration of Principles jointly adopted by a Committee of the American Bar Association and a Committee of Publishers.

Published by Sphinx Publishing, a division of Sphinx International, Inc., Post Office Box 25, Clearwater, Florida 34617-0025. This publication is available by mail for $9.95 plus $3.00 for first class Priority Mail.

Table of Contents

Introduction 5

Using Self-Help Law Books 6

Chapter 1 Basic Rules You Should Know 7
What is a Will?
A Will is Part of Probate
Joint Tenancy Overrules a Will and Avoids Probate
"Tenancy in Common" Does Not Avoid Probate
A Spouse Can Overrule a Will
Joint Tenancy Overrules a Spouse's Share
Joint Tenancy is Risky
I/T/F Bank Accounts Are Better Than Joint Ownership
Totten Trust is not Applicable in Securities in Massachusetts
Getting Married Automatically Changes Your Will
Having Children Automatically Changes Your Will
Getting Divorced Automatically Changes Your Will

Chapter 2 Do You Need a Massachusetts Will?
What a Will Can Do
What If You Have No Will?
Is Your Out of State Will Good in Massachusetts?
Who Can Make a Massachusetts Will?
What a Will Cannot Do
Who Can Use a Simple Will
Who Should Not Use a Simple Will

Chapter 3 How To Make a Simple Will 19
Identifying People in Your Will
Personal Property
Specific Bequests
Remainder Clause
Alternate Beneficiaries
Survivorship
Guardians
Executor/Executrix
Witnesses

Self-Proving Clause
Funeral Arrangements
Miscellaneous
Forms

Chapter 4 How To Execute a Will 25

Chapter 5 After You Sign Your Will 27
Storing Your Will
Revoking Your Will
Changing Your Will

Chapter 6 How To Make a Living Will and Health Care Proxy 29

Chapter 7 How To Make Anatomical Gifts 31

Appendix A Forms (2 copies of each) 33
A. Simple Will - Property to Spouse **or** Adult Children, 35, 37
B. Simple Will - Property to Spouse **or** Minor Children - One Guardian, 39, 41
C. Simple Will - Property to Spouse **or** Minor Children - Two Guardians, 43, 45
D. Simple Will - Property to Spouse **or** Minor Children - Guardian and Trust, 47, 49
E. Simple Will - Property to Spouse **and** Adult Children, 51, 53
F. Simple Will - Property to Spouse **and** Others, 55, 57
G. Simple Will - (No Spouse) - Property to Minor Children - One Guardian, 59, 61
H. Simple Will - (No Spouse) - Property to Minor Children - Two Guardians, 63, 65
I. Simple Will - (No Spouse) - Property to Minor Children - Guardian and Trust, 67, 69
J. Simple Will - (No Spouse - No Minor Children), 71, 73
K. Self-Proved Will Page, 75, 77
L. Codicil to Will, 79, 81
M. Living Will and Health Care Proxy, 83, 85
N. Organ Donor Card, 87

Appendix B Sample Filled-in Forms 89

Index 96

Introduction

This book is intended to give Massachusetts residents a basic understanding of the laws regarding wills, joint property and other types of ownership of property as they affect their estate planning. It is designed to allow those with simple estates to quickly and inexpensively set up their affairs to distribute their property according to their wishes.

It also includes information on appointing a guardian for minor children. This can be useful in avoiding bad feelings between relatives and in protecting the children from being raised by someone you would object to obtaining custody.

Chapters 1 through 7 explain the laws which control wills. Appendix A contains blank will forms you can cut out or photocopy. Appendix B contains some sample filled-in will forms to show you how it is done.

You can prepare your own will quickly and easily by using the forms out of the book, or by photocopying them, or you can retype the material on blank paper. The small amount of time it takes to do this can give you and your heirs the peace of mind of knowing that your estate will be distributed according to your wishes.

A surprising number of people have had their estates pass to the wrong parties because of a simple lack of knowledge of what they were doing. Before using any of the forms in Appendix A, you should read and understand the previous chapters of this book.

In each example given you might ask, "What if the spouse died first?" or "What if the children were grown?" and then the answer might be different. If your situation is at all complicated you are advised to seek the advice of an attorney. In many communities wills are available for very reasonable prices. No book of this type can cover every contingency in every case, but a knowledge of the basics will help you to make the right decisions regarding your property.

Using Self-Help Law Books

Whenever you shop for a product or service, you are faced with a variety of different levels of quality and price. In deciding what to buy, you make a cost/value analysis on the basis of your willingness to pay and the quality you desire.

When buying a car, you decide whether you want transportation, comfort, status, or sex appeal, and you decide among such choices as a Neon, a Lincoln, a Rolls Royce, or a Porsche. Before making a decision, you usually weigh the merits of each against the cost.

When you get a headache, you can take a pain reliever such as aspirin or you can go to a medical specialist for a neurological examination. Given this choice, most people, of course, take a pain reliever, since it costs only pennies, whereas a medical examination costs hundreds of dollars and takes a lot of time. This is usually a logical choice because rarely is anything more than a pain reliever needed for a headache. But in some cases a headache may indicate a brain tumor, and failing to go to a specialist right away can result in complications. Should everyone with a headache go to a specialist? Of course not, but people treating their own illnesses must realize that they are betting on the basis of their cost/value analysis of the situation, that they are taking the most logical option.

The same cost/value analysis must be made in deciding to do one's own legal work. Many legal situations are very simple, requiring a simple form and no complicated analysis. Anyone with a little intelligence and a book of instructions can handle the matter simply.

But there is always the chance that there is a complication involved that only a lawyer would notice. To simplify the law into a book like this, several legal cases often must be condensed into a single sentence or paragraph. Otherwise, the book would be several hundred pages long and too complicated for most people. However, this simplification necessarily leaves out many details and nuances that would apply to special or unusual situations. Also, there are many ways to interpret most legal questions. Your case may come before a judge who disagrees with the analysis of our author.

Therefore, in deciding to use a self-help law book and to do your own legal work, you must realize that you are making a cost/value analysis and deciding that the chance that your case will not turn out to your satisfaction is outweighed by the money you will save by doing it yourself. Most people handling their own simple legal matters never have a problem, but occasionally people find that it ended up costing them more to have an attorney straighten out the situation than it would have if they had hired an attorney to begin with. Keep this in mind while handling your case, and be sure to consult an attorney if you feel you might need further guidance.

There is no worse torture than the torture of laws.

—Francis Bacon

Chapter 1
Basic Rules You Should Know

What is a Will?

A will is a document you can use to control who gets your property, who will be guardian of your children and who will manage your estate.

A Will is Part of Probate

Some people think a will avoids probate. It does not. A will is the document used in probate to determine who receives the property or is appointed guardian or executor.

If you wish to avoid probate you need to use methods other than a will, such as joint ownership, pay-on-death accounts or living trusts. The first two of these are discussed later in this chapter. For information on living trusts you should check with your bookstore or the publisher.

If a person successfully avoids probate with all of his or her property, then he or she may not need a will. However, everyone should have a will in case some property, which was forgotten or received just prior to death, does not avoid probate for some reason.

Joint Tenancy Overrules a Will and Avoids Probate

Where a will gives property to one person but it is already in a joint account with another person, the will is ignored and the joint owner of the account gets the property. This is because the property in the account avoids probate and passes directly to the joint owner. A will only controls property which goes through probate. There are exceptions to this rule. If some money is put into a joint account only for convenience it might pass under the will, but if the joint owner does not give it up, it could take an expensive court battle to get it back.

Examples:

1. Bill's will leaves all his property to his wife, Mary. Bill dies owning a house jointly with his sister, Joan, and a bank account jointly with his son, Don. Joan gets the house, Don gets the bank account and his wife, Mary, gets nothing.

2. Betty's will leaves half her assets to Ann and half her assets to George. Betty dies owning $1,000,000 in stock jointly with George and a car in her own name. Ann gets only a half interest in the car. George gets all the stock and half the car.

3. John's will leaves all his property equally to his five children. Before going in the hospital he puts his oldest son, Harry, as a joint owner of his accounts. John dies and Harry gets all of his assets. The rest of the children get nothing.

In each of these cases the property went to a person it probably shouldn't have because the decedent didn't realize that joint ownership overruled their will. In some families this might not be a problem. Harry might divide up the property equally (and possibly pay a gift tax.) But in many cases Harry would just keep everything and the family would never talk to him again.

"Tenancy in Common" Does Not Avoid Probate

In Massachusetts there are three basic ways to own property, joint tenancy with right of survivorship, tenancy in common and tenancy by the entirety. Joint tenancy with right of survivorship means when one owner of the property dies the survivor automatically gets the decedent's share. Tenancy in common means when one owner dies, that owner's share of the property goes to his or her heirs under the will. A tenancy by the entirety is like joint tenancy with right of survivorship, but it can only apply to a married couple.

Examples: 1.   Tom and Marcia bought a house and lived together for 20 years. But the deed did not specify joint tenancy. When Tom died his brother inherited his half of the house and it had to be sold because Marcia could not afford to buy it from him.

2.   Lindsay and her husband Rocky bought a house. When Rocky suddenly died Lindsay obtained full ownership of the house by filing a death certificate at the courthouse. That was because the deed to the house stated that they were husband and wife so ownership was presumed to be tenancy by the entireties.

A Spouse Can Overrule a Will

Under Massachusetts law, a surviving spouse, upon waiver of the will, is entitled to a minimum share of the decedent's estate no matter what the will says. This is sometimes called the "forced share" or "elective share." The amount of the forced share varies depending on whether the decedent also leaves issue and/or kin.

If Issue Survive: If issue (i.e., children, grandchildren, or great grandchildren) survive, then the surviving spouse is entitled to one-third of the personal property and one-third of the real property (house) in the estate. If, however, the forced share would exceed $25,000.00, the spouse is then entitled to real or personal property worth $25,000.00 and a life interest in the amount by which that one-third share exceeds the $25,000.00.

If Only Kin Survive: If the decedent only leaves kin and no issue, then the surviving spouse, upon waiver of the will, is entitled to $25,000.00 outright and a life interest in one-half of the remaining personal property and one-half of the remaining real property.

If No Issue or Kin Survive: If the decedent does not leave issue or kin, then the surviving spouse, upon waiver of the will, is entitled to $25,000.00 plus one-half of the remaining personal property and real property outright.

Examples:
1. John's will leaves all of his property (worth $18,000.00) to his children of a prior marriage and nothing to his wife who is already wealthy. Since issue survive, the wife, by waiving the will, gets one-third, or $6,000.00.

2. Mary, who is married but without children, puts half of her property in a joint account with husband and in her will she leaves all of her property to her sister who is ill. When she dies her husband gets all the money in the joint account and $25,000.00 outright with a life-interest in one-half of both the remaining real and personal property.

Joint Tenancy Overrules a Spouse's Share

One way to avoid a spouse's forced share is to have all property in joint ownership with others. Other ways are to sign an agreement with your spouse either before or after the marriage or to set up a trust.

Example:
Dan owns his stocks jointly with his son. He owns his bank accounts jointly with his daughter. If he has no other property his spouse gets nothing since there is no property in his estate.

Joint Tenancy is Risky

The above cases may make it appear that joint tenancy is the answer to all problems, but it often creates even more problems. If you put your real estate in joint ownership with someone, you cannot sell it or mortgage it without that person's signature. If you put your bank account in joint ownership with someone they can take out all of your money.

Examples: 1.   Alice put her house in joint ownership with her son. She later married Ed and moved in with him. She wanted to sell her house and to invest the money for income. Her son refused to sign the deed. She was in court for ten months getting her house back and the judge almost refused to do it.

2.   Alex put his bank accounts into joint ownership with his daughter Mary to avoid probate. Mary fell in love with Doug who was in trouble with the law. Doug talked Mary into "borrowing" $30,000 from the account for a "business deal" that went sour. Later she "borrowed" $25,000 more to pay Doug's bail bond. Alex didn't find out until it was too late that his money was gone.

I/T/F Bank Accounts are Better Than Joint Ownership

One way to keep bank accounts out of your estate and still retain control is to title them "In Trust For" or I/T/F and name a beneficiary. Some banks may use the letters POD for "pay on death" or TOD for "transfer on death." Either way the result is the same. No one except you can get the money until your death, and on death it immediately goes directly to the person you name without a will or probate proceeding. These are what are called "Totten Trusts" after the man who had to go to court to prove they were legal.

Example: Rich opened a bank account in the name of "Rich, I/T/F Mary." If Rich dies the money automatically goes to Mary, but prior to his death Mary has no control over the account, doesn't even have to know about it, and Rich can take Mary's name off the account at any time.

Totten Trust is Not Applicable to Securities in Massachusetts

The drawback of the Totten Trust is that it is only good for cash in a bank account. In Massachusetts, stocks and bonds, unless held in an Individual Retirement Account (IRA) or by joint tenancy, still must go through probate. While other states have passed laws allowing stocks, bonds, and securities accounts to also transfer automatically on death, Massachusetts has yet to follow suit.

In Massachusetts, however, the law does allow for the change of registration of the securities upon death in certain situations. If the owner of securities cumulatively valued at no more than $2,100.00 dies, his or her spouse (or adult child or parent if no spouse) may arrange to have the securities registered in his or her name. In order for this to be allowed, thirty days must have elapsed since the decedent's death without the executor or administrator of the estate making written demand to the security issuer for payment.

Getting Married Automatically Changes Your Will

If you get married after making your will and do not rewrite it after the wedding, your spouse gets a share of your estate as if you had no will unless you have a pre-nuptial agreement, or you made a provision for your spouse in the will.

Example: John made out his will leaving his modest estate to his disabled brother. When he married Joan, an heiress with plenty of money, he didn't change his will because he still wanted his brother to get his estate. When he died, Joan got his entire estate and his brother got nothing.

Having Children Automatically Changes Your Will

If you have a child after making your will and do not rewrite it, the child gets a share of your estate as if there was no will.

Example: Dave made a will leaving half his estate to his sister and the other half to be shared by his three children. He later has another child and doesn't revise his will. Upon his death, his four children would share equally one-half of the estate (one-eighth for each child) and the sister would receive the other half of the estate (four-eighths).

Getting Divorced Automatically Changes Your Will

If, after executing a will, you become divorced or your marriage is annulled, the divorce or annulment voids any property which passes to your ex- spouse as if your ex-spouse predeceased you. Divorce and annulment also revokes any provision in the will which nominates the ex-spouse as executor, trustee, conservator, or guardian. A separation, on the other hand, does not revoke any of the spouse's provisions in the will.

Example: Carol, during her marriage to Jim, executed a will leaving everything to him, and if Jim predeceased her, then everything to her children. One year after the will was executed, Carol divorced Jim and never changed her will. Five years later, Carol died. Her children would receive everything under her will.

There are two things in which men, in other things wise enough, do usually miscarry; in putting off the making of their wills and their repentance until it is too late.
—Tillotson

Chapter 2
Do You Need a Massachusetts Will?

What a Will Can Do

1. A will allows you to decide who gets your property after your death. You can give specific personal items to certain persons and decide which of your friends or relatives deserve a greater share of your estate. You can leave gifts to schools and charities.

2. A will allows you to decide who will be the Executor (or Executrix) of your estate. An Executor is the person who gathers together all your assets and distributes them to the beneficiaries. With a will you can provide that your Executor does not have to post a surety bond with the court in order to serve and this can save your estate some money.

3. A will allows you to choose a guardian for your minor children. This way you can avoid fights among relatives and make sure the best person raises your children. You may also appoint separate guardians over your children and over their money. For example you may appoint your sister as guardian over your children and your father as guardian over their money. That way a second person could keep an eye on how their money was being spent.

4. You can set up a trust to provide that your property is not distributed immediately. Many people feel that their children would not be ready to handle large sums of money at the age of eighteen. A will can direct that the money is held until the children are 21 or 25 or older.

What If You Have No Will?

If you do not have a will, Massachusetts law says that your property shall be distributed as follows:

1. If you leave a spouse and no children or issue, your spouse gets your entire estate if the whole estate does not exceed two hundred thousand dollars in value. If it is greater than $200,000, the spouse takes $200,000 plus half of the remainder of the estate.

2. If you leave a spouse and at least one child (or issue) then your spouse gets half of your estate and your children get equal shares of the other half.

3. If you leave no spouse, all of your children get equal shares of your estate. If one of your children predeceases you but leaves children of his own, then those children will share equally in their parent's share.

4. If you leave no spouse and no children then your estate would go to the highest persons on the following list who are living.

    a. Your parents

    b. Your brothers and sisters, or if dead, their children

    c. Next of kin in equal degree. If there are two or more collateral kindred in equal degree claiming through different ancestors, those claiming through the nearest ancestor shall be preferred.

5. If you die without a will and leave no spouse and no kindred, then your property is transferred ("escheats") to the Commonwealth of Massachusetts.

Is Your Out-of-State Will Good in Massachusetts?

A will that is valid in another state would probably be valid to pass property in Massachusetts. However, if the will is not "self-proved," before it could be accepted by a Massachusetts Probate Court a person in your former state would have to be appointed as a "Commissioner" to take the oath of a person who witnessed your signature on the will. Because of the expense and delay in having a Commissioner appointed and the problems in finding out-of-state witnesses, it is advisable to execute a new will after moving to Massachusetts.

Massachusetts also allows a will to be "self-proved" so that the witnesses never have to be called in to take an oath. With special self-proving language in your will the witnesses take the oath at the time of signing and never have to be seen again.

Who Can Make a Massachusetts Will?

Any person who is 18 or more years of age and of sound mind.

What a Will Cannot Do

A will cannot direct that anything illegal be done and it cannot put unreasonable conditions on a gift. A provision that your daughter gets all of your property if she divorces her husband would be ignored by the court. She would get the property either way.

Who Can Use a Simple Will

 If your estate is under $600,000.00 and you wish to divide up your property simply you can use a simple will. If you want to put any complicated terms in your will, or if you wish to leave your spouse or any of your children out of your will, you should consult a lawyer to be sure that the terms are drawn properly and are enforceable.

Who Should Not Use a Simple Will

If you expect that there may be a fight over your will or that someone might contest its validity you should consult a lawyer. If you are the beneficiary of a trust or have any complications in your legal relationships you may need special provisions in your will. A person who can sign only with an "X" should also consult a lawyer. If you expect to have over $600,000.00 at the time of your death, you may want to consult with a CPA or tax attorney regarding tax consequences.

What you leave at your death let it be without controversy, else the lawyers will be your heirs.

—F. Osborn

Chapter 3
How to Make a Simple Will

Identifying People in Your Will

When making your will it is important to correctly identify the persons you name in your will. In some families names differ only by middle initial or by Jr. or Sr. Be sure to check the names before you make your will. You can also add your relationship to the party, and their location such as *"my cousin, Laura Jones of Saugus, Massachusetts"* The same applies to organizations and charities. For example there are more than one group using the words "cancer society" or "heart association" in their names. Be sure to get the correct name of the group to which you intend to leave your gift.

Personal Property

Because people acquire and dispose of personal property so often, it is not advisable to list each item in the will. Massachusetts law allows you to include a handwritten list with your will which can divide up your personal property if the list is referred to in the will. This only applies to "tangible personal property" such as watches, photos, cars, furniture, jewelry, etc. It does not include money, stocks, bonds or real estate. By using such a list you can have the flexibility to make changes when you acquire or dispose of property, such as buying a new car or jewelry items. Be sure to clearly identify each item on your list so there is no confusion.

Specific Bequests

Occasionally a person will want to leave a little something to a friend or charity and the rest to the family. This can be done with a "specific bequest" such as *"$1,000 to my dear friend Martha Jones."* Of course there could be a problem if, at the time of a person's death, there wasn't anything left after the specific bequests.

Remainder Clause

In a simple will it is not advisable to give specific property. If some property has been sold or declines in value by the time of your death, one beneficiary may not get the amount you intended. It is more common to list a percentage for each beneficiary. That way if your property changes over the years it will still be divided fairly.

Example: Joe wanted his children to equally share his estate. His will left his son his stocks (worth $500,000 at the time) and his daughter $500,000 in cash. By the time of Joe's death the stock was only worth $100,000. He should have left 50% of his estate to each child.

If it is an important part of your estate plan, you can give specific items to specific persons, but remember to make changes if your assets change.

Alternate Beneficiaries

You should always provide for an alternate beneficiary in case the first one dies before you do and you do not have a chance to make out a new will.

If you are giving property to two or more persons and if you want it all to go to the other if one of them dies, then you would specify *"or the survivor of them."*

If, on the other hand, you want the property to go to the children of the deceased person you should state in your will, "or their lineal descendants" of the person. This would include his or her children and grandchildren. In naming lineal descendants you must decide whether the property shall pass "per stirpes" or "per capita." Per stirpes means that each *branch* of the family gets an equal share. Per capita means that each *person* gets an equal share.

Example: Alice leaves her property to her two daughters, Mary and Pat in equal shares, or to their lineal descendants *per stirpes*. Both daughters die before Alice. Mary leaves one child, Pat leaves two children. In this case Mary's child would get half of the estate and Pat's children would split the other half of the estate. If Alice had specified *per capita* instead of *per stirpes* then each child would have gotten one-third of the estate.

Per Stirpes Distribution

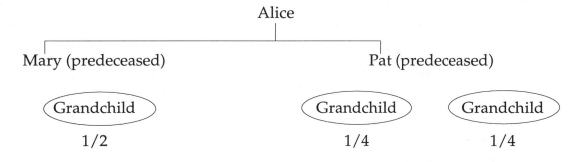

Per Capita Distribution

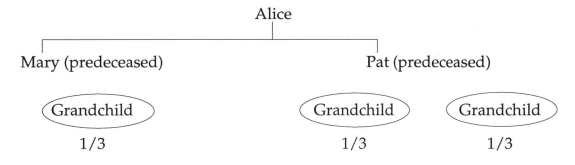

There are 14 different forms in this book, but you may want to divide your property slightly differently from what is stated in these forms. If so, you can re-type the forms according to these rules, specifying whether the property should go to the survivor or the lineal descendants. If this is confusing to you, you should consider seeking the advice of an attorney.

Survivorship

Many people put a clause in their will stating that anyone receiving property under the will must survive for 30 days (or 45 or 60) after the death of the deceased. This is so that if the two people die in the same accident there will not be two probates and the property will not go to the other party's heirs.

Example: Fred and Wilma were married and each had children by previous marriages. They didn't have survivorship clauses in their wills and they were in an airplane crash. Fred's children hired several expert witnesses and a large law firm to prove that at the time of the crash Fred lived for a few minutes longer than Wilma. That way when Wilma died first all of her property went to Fred. When he died a few minutes later all of Fred and Wilma's property went to his children and Wilma's children got nothing.

Guardians

If you have minor children you should name a guardian for them. There are two types of guardians, a guardian over the "person" and a guardian over the "property." The first is the person who decides where the children will live and makes the other parental decisions for them. A guardian of the property is in charge of the minor's property and inheritance. In most cases one person is appointed guardian of both the person and property. But some people prefer the children to live with one person but to have the money held by another person.

When naming a guardian, it is always advisable to name an alternate guardian in case your first choice is unable to serve for any reason.

Executor/Executrix

An Executor (Executrix if a woman) is the person who will be in charge of your probate. He or she will gather your assets, handle the sale of them if necessary, prepare an inventory, hire an attorney and distribute the property. It should be a person you trust and, if it is, then you can state in your will that no bond will be required to be posted by him or her. Otherwise the court will require that a surety bond be paid for by your estate to guaranty that the Executor is honest. You can appoint a bank as your Executor but their fees are usually very high.

It is best to have a Massachusetts resident as an Executor both because it is easier and because a bond may be required of a non-resident even if your will waives it.

Some people like to name two persons as Co-Executors to avoid jealousy, or for other reasons. However, this is not a good idea. It makes double work in getting the papers signed and there can be problems if they cannot agree on something.

Witnesses

A will must be witnessed by two persons to be valid in Massachusetts. In some states, such as Louisiana, three witnesses are required, so if you own property in other states you should have three witnesses to your will. In some states a will that is entirely handwritten is valid if there are no witnesses, but in Massachusetts a will would be invalid without the witnesses.

In Massachusetts, the witnesses to your will, or their spouses, are not allowed to receive property from your will unless there are two other subscribing witnesses to the will who do not likewise benefit.

Self-Proving Clause

A will only needs two witnesses to be legal, but if there is also a notary and a self-proving clause is signed, it can be admitted to probate much faster. Without this clause one of the witnesses has to go to the courthouse and sign an oath. This can cause a delay in probating your estate if the witness cannot get to the courthouse right away. With this clause it can be immediately accepted by the court even if both witnesses are dead.

Funeral Arrangements

There is no harm in stating your preferences in your will but directions for a funeral are not legally enforceable and many times a will is not found until after the funeral. Therefore it is better to tell your family about your wishes or to make prior arrangements yourself.

Miscellaneous

Your will can be entirely typed, handwritten or filled-in on a form. It should have no white-outs or erasures. If for some reason it is impossible to make a will without corrections, they should be initialed by you and both witnesses. If there are two or more pages they should be fastened together and each page should be initialed.

Forms

There are several different forms included in this book for easy use. You can either cut them out or photocopy them, or you can retype them on plain paper.

One eye-witness is worth more than ten who tell what they have heard.
                                        —Plautus, c. 254 - 184 B.C.

Chapter 4
How to Execute a Will

The signing of a will is a serious legal event and must be done properly or the will may be declared invalid. Preferably it should be done in a private room without distraction. All parties must watch each other sign and no one should leave the scene until all have signed.

Example: Ebenezer was sick in bed in a small room. When he signed his will the witnesses could not actually see his hand because the dresser was in the way. His will was ignored by the court and his property went to persons not named in the will.

Procedures: The person signing the will (the Testator) and the two witnesses should be able to see each other and the will. The Testator should state, "This is my will. I have read it and I understand it and this is how I want it to read. I want you two people to be my witnesses." Then the Testator and the witnesses should watch each other sign.

For a self-proved will a notary public should also be present and watch the signing. Then the parties should swear to the statements in the self-proving clause and sign again. Then the notary should sign and seal the will and write in the expiration date of his or her notary commission.

It is a good idea to make a least one copy of your will, but you should not sign or notarize the copies. The reason for this is if you cancel or intentionally destroy your original will someone might bring out a copy and say that it is the original.

If someone made a mistake he would drawl, "Hell, that's why they make erasers."
—Clarence Darrow

Chapter 5
After You Sign Your Will

Storing Your Will

Your will should be kept in a place safe from fire and easily accessible to your heirs. Your Executor should know of its whereabouts. It can be kept in a home safe or fire box or in a safe deposit box in a bank. In some states a will should not be placed in a safe deposit box because they are sealed at death, but in Massachusetts it is easy to get a will out of a deceased person's safe deposit box.

Wills are not filed anywhere until after a person's death. No one has to know what you have put in your will while you are alive. Often an attorney preparing a will will offer to keep it in his safe deposit box at no charge. This way he or she will likely be contacted at the time of death and will be in a good position to do the lucrative probate work.

Revoking Your Will

A person who has made a will may revoke it or may direct someone else to revoke it in his presence. This may be done by burning, tearing, cancelling, defacing, obliterating or destroying it with the intention and for the purpose of revoking it. Revoking one will does not revive older wills which have been replaced by the revoked will.

Example: Ralph tells his son Clyde to go to the basement safe and tear up his (Ralph's) will. If Clyde does not tear it up in Ralph's presence it is probably not effectively revoked.

Changing Your Will

You should not make any changes on your will after it has been signed. If you wish to change some provision of your will, you can do it by executing a document called a "codicil." A person may make an unlimited number of codicils to a will, but each one must be executed with the same formality of a will and should be self-proved. Therefore, it is usually better to just prepare a new will than to prepare codicils.

Confidence in others' honesty is no light testimony of one's own integrity.
—Michel de Montaigne

Chapter 6
How to Make a Living Will and Health Care Proxy

In 1990, the Massachusetts legislature passed a "living will" law which allows a person who is at least eighteen years old ("the principal") to appoint another person as his or her "health care agent", authorizing this agent to make the principal's medical decisions when and if the principal becomes incapacitated. The health care proxy must be in writing, signed by the principal, and witnessed by two people, each of whom can not be the designated health care agent.

A health care proxy must: 1) identify the principal and the health care agent; 2) indicate that the principal intends the agent to have authority to make health care decisions on the principal's behalf; 3) describe the limitation, if any, that the principal intends to impose upon the agent's authority; and 4) indicate that the agent's authority shall become effective if it is determined that the principal lacks capacity to make health care decisions.

The health care agent may make any decisions regarding medical treatment that the principal could make, including decisions about life-sustaining treatment, subject, however, to any express limitations in the health care proxy. A person, in a "Living Will" may expressly state his or her desire not to be kept alive by any artificial life support.

A living will and health care proxy form is included in Appendix A of this book.

Behold, I do not give lectures or a little charity, When I give I give myself.
—Walt Whitman, *Leaves of Grass*

Chapter 7
How to Make Anatomical Gifts

Massachusetts allows its residents to donate their bodies or organs for research or transplantation. Consent may be given by a relative of a deceased person but, because relatives are often in shock or too upset to make such a decision, it is better to have one's intent made clear before death. This can be done by a statement in a will or by another signed document such as a Uniform Donor Card. The gift may be of all or part of one's body, and it may be made to a specific person such as a physician or an ill relative.

The document making the donation must be signed before two witnesses who must also sign in each other's presence. If the donor cannot sign then the document may be signed for him at his direction in the presence of the witnesses.

The donor may designate in the document who the physician is who will carry out the procedure.

If the document or will has been delivered to a specific donee it may be amended or revoked by the donor in the following ways:

1.   By executing and delivering a signed statement to the donee.

2.   By an oral statement to two witnesses communicated to the donee.

3.   By an oral statement during a terminal illness made to an attending physician and communicated to the donee.

4.   By a signed document found on the person of the donor or in his or her effects.

If a document of gift has not been delivered to a donee it may be revoked by any of the above methods or by destruction, cancellation or mutilation of the document. If the gift is made by a will, it may be revoked in the same method a will is revoked as described on page 29.

A Uniform Donor Card is included in Appendix A as Form N. It must be signed in the presence of two signing witnesses.

Appendix A - Forms

The following pages contain forms which can be used to prepare a will, codicil, living will and Uniform Donor Card. They should only be used by persons who have read this book, who do not have any complications in their legal affairs and who understand the forms they are using. The forms may be used right out of the book or they may be photocopied or retyped. Two copies are included of each form.

Form A. Simple Will - Property to Spouse **or** Adult Children. *This will should be used by persons who want all of their property to go to their spouse, but if the spouse has died previously, then to their children, all of whom are adults. (Pages 35 and 37)*

Form B. Simple Will - Property to Spouse **or** Minor Children - One Guardian. *This will should be used by persons who have minor children and want all their property to go to their spouse, but if the spouse has died previously, then to their minor children. It provides for one person to be guardian over the children and their estates. (Pages 39 and 41)*

Form C. Simple Will - Property to Spouse **or** Minor Children - Two Guardians. *This will should be used by persons who have minor children and want all their property to go to their spouse, but if the spouse has died previously, then to their minor children. It provides for two guardians, one over the children and one over their estates. (Pages 43 and 45)*

Form D. Simple Will - Property to Spouse **or** Minor Children - Guardian and Trust. *This will should be used by persons who have minor children and want all their property to go to their spouse, but if the spouse has died previously, then to their minor children. It provides for one person to be guardian over the children and for either the same person or another to be trustee over their property. This will allows the children's property to be held until they are older than 18 rather than distributing it all to them at age 18. (Pages 47 and 49)*

Form E. Simple Will - Property to Spouse **and** Adult Children. *This will should be used by persons who want their property to go to both their spouse and to their adult children. (Pages 51 and 53)*

Form F. Simple Will - Property to Spouse **and** Others. *This will should be used by persons who want their property to go to both their spouse and to other parties. (Pages 55 and 57)*

Form G. Simple Will - (No Spouse) - Property to Minor Children - One Guardian. *This will is for persons who do not have a spouse and want all their property to go to their children, at least one of whom is a minor. It provides for one person to be guardian over the children and their estates. (Pages 59 and 61)*

Form H. Simple Will - (No Spouse) - Property to Minor Children - Two Guardians. *This will is for persons who do not have a spouse and want all their property to go to their children, at least one of whom is a minor. It provides for two guardians, one over the children and one over their estates. (Pages 63 and 65)*

Form I. Simple Will - (No Spouse) - Property to Minor Children - Guardian and Trust. *This will is for persons who do not have a spouse and want all their property to go to their children, at least one of whom is a minor. It provides for one person to be guardian over the children and for either that person or another to be trustee over their property. This will allows the children's property to be held until they are older than 18 rather than distributing it all to them at age 18. (Pages 67 and 69)*

Form J. Simple Will - (No Spouse - No Minor Children) *This will should be used by persons who wish to leave their property to persons or entities other than a spouse or minor children. (Pages 71 and 73)*

Form K. Self-Proved Will Page - *This page should be attached to every will as the final page. It must be witnessed and notarized. (Pages 75 and 77)*

Form L. Codicil to Will - *This form can be used to change one section of a will. Usually it is just as easy to execute a new will, since all of the same formalities are required. (Pages 79 and 81)*

Form M. Living Will and Health Care Proxy- *This form is used to state that you do not want your life artificially prolonged if you have a terminal illness. (Pages 83 and 85)*

Form N. Organ Donor Card. *This form is used to spell out your wishes for donation of your body or any organs. (Page 87)*

Last Will and Testament

I, _____ a resident of _____ , Massachusetts do hereby make, publish and declare this to be my Last Will and Testament, hereby revoking any and all Wills and Codicils heretofore made by me.

FIRST: I direct that all my just debts and funeral expenses be paid out of my estate as soon after my death as is practicable.

SECOND: I may leave a statement or list disposing of certain items of my tangible personal property. Any such statement or list in existence at the time of my death shall be determinative with respect to all items bequeathed therein.

THIRD: All the rest, residue and remainder of my estate, real or personal, wheresoever situate, now owned or hereafter acquired by me, which at the time of my death shall belong to me or be subject to my disposal by Will, I give devise and bequeath unto my spouse, _____ .

FOURTH: In the event that my said spouse predeceases me, or fails to survive me by thirty days, then I give devise and bequeath the rest, residue and remainder of my estate unto my children, _____ _____ .

FIFTH: I hereby nominate, constitute and appoint _____ to serve as Executor (Executrix) of this, my Last Will and Testament, to serve without bond or surety. In the event that he or she is unable or unwilling to serve at any time or for any reason then I nominate, constitute and appoint _____ as alternate Executor (Executrix) also to serve without bond or surety. I give my said Executor (Executrix) the fullest power in all matters including the power to sell or convey real or personal property or any interest therein without court order.

IN WITNESS WHEREOF I have signed and published this my Last Will and Testament this _____ day of _____ , 19____ .

_____ L.S.

The foregoing Instrument was signed by _____ as his/her Last Will and Testament in our presence and we in his/her presence and in each other's presence have signed the same as witnesses thereto.

_____ residing at_____

_____ residing at_____

Last Will and Testament

I, _____ a resident of _____ , Massachusetts do hereby make, publish and declare this to be my Last Will and Testament, hereby revoking any and all Wills and Codicils heretofore made by me.

FIRST: I direct that all my just debts and funeral expenses be paid out of my estate as soon after my death as is practicable.

SECOND: I may leave a statement or list disposing of certain items of my tangible personal property. Any such statement or list in existence at the time of my death shall be determinative with respect to all items bequeathed therein.

THIRD: All the rest, residue and remainder of my estate, real or personal, wheresoever situate, now owned or hereafter acquired by me, which at the time of my death shall belong to me or be subject to my disposal by Will, I give devise and bequeath unto my spouse, _____.

FOURTH: In the event that my said spouse predeceases me, or fails to survive me by thirty days, then I give devise and bequeath the rest, residue and remainder of my estate unto my children, _____ _____.

FIFTH: I hereby nominate, constitute and appoint _____ to serve as Executor (Executrix) of this, my Last Will and Testament, to serve without bond or surety. In the event that he or she is unable or unwilling to serve at any time or for any reason then I nominate, constitute and appoint _____ as alternate Executor (Executrix) also to serve without bond or surety. I give my said Executor (Executrix) the fullest power in all matters including the power to sell or convey real or personal property or any interest therein without court order.

IN WITNESS WHEREOF I have signed and published this my Last Will and Testament this _____ day of _____, 19____.

_____L.S.

The foregoing Instrument was signed by _____ as his/her Last Will and Testament in our presence and we in his/her presence and in each other's presence have signed the same as witnesses thereto.

_____residing at_____

_____residing at_____

Last Will and Testament

I, _____ a resident of _____ County, Massachusetts do hereby make, publish and declare this to be my Last Will and Testament, hereby revoking any and all Wills and Codicils heretofore made by me.

FIRST: I direct that all my just debts and funeral expenses be paid out of my estate as soon after my death as is practicable.

SECOND: I may leave a statement or list disposing of certain items of my tangible personal property. Any such statement or list in existence at the time of my death shall be determinative with respect to all items bequeathed therein.

THIRD: All the rest, residue and remainder of my estate, real or personal, wheresoever situate, now owned or hereafter acquired by me, which at the time of my death shall belong to me or be subject to my disposal by Will, I give devise and bequeath unto my spouse, _____.

FOURTH: In the event that my said spouse predeceases me, or fails to survive me by thirty days, then I give devise and bequeath the rest, residue and remainder of my estate unto my children, _____
_____.

FIFTH: I hereby nominate, constitute and appoint _____ as guardian over the person and estate of any of my children who have not reached the age of majority at the time of my death. In the event that said guardian is unable or unwilling to serve then I nominate, constitute and appoint _____ as guardian.

SIXTH: I hereby nominate, constitute and appoint _____ to serve as Executor (Executrix) of this, my Last Will and Testament, to serve without bond or surety. In the event that he or she is unable or unwilling to serve at any time for any reason then I nominate, constitute and appoint _____ as alternate Executor (Executrix) also to serve without bond or surety. I give my said Executor (Executrix) the fullest power in all matters including the power to sell or convey real or personal property or any interest therein without court order.

IN WITNESS WHEREOF I have signed and published this my Last Will and Testament this _____ day of _____, 19____.

_____L.S.

The foregoing instrument was signed by _____ as his/her Last Will and Testament in our presence and we in his/her presence and in each other's presence have signed the same as witnesses thereto.

_____residing at_____

_____residing at_____

Last Will and Testament

I, _____ a resident of _____ , Massachusetts do hereby make, publish and declare this to be my Last Will and Testament, hereby revoking any and all Wills and Codicils heretofore made by me.

FIRST: I direct that all my just debts and funeral expenses be paid out of my estate as soon after my death as is practicable.

SECOND: I may leave a statement or list disposing of certain items of my tangible personal property. Any such statement or list in existence at the time of my death shall be determinative with respect to all items bequeathed therein.

THIRD: All the rest, residue and remainder of my estate, real or personal, wheresoever situate, now owned or hereafter acquired by me, which at the time of my death shall belong to me or be subject to my disposal by Will, I give devise and bequeath unto my spouse, _____.

FOURTH: In the event that my said spouse predeceases me, or fails to survive me by thirty days, then I give devise and bequeath the rest, residue and remainder of my estate unto my children, _____ _____.

FIFTH: I hereby nominate, constitute and appoint _____ as guardian over the person and estate of any of my children who have not reached the age of majority at the time of my death. In the event that said guardian is unable or unwilling to serve then I nominate, constitute and appoint _____ as guardian.

SIXTH: I hereby nominate, constitute and appoint _____ to serve as Executor (Executrix) of this, my Last Will and Testament, to serve without bond or surety. In the event that he or she is unable or unwilling to serve at any time for any reason then I nominate, constitute and appoint _____ as alternate Executor (Executrix) also to serve without bond or surety. I give my said Executor (Executrix) the fullest power in all matters including the power to sell or convey real or personal property or any interest therein without court order.

IN WITNESS WHEREOF I have signed and published this my Last Will and Testament this _____ day of _____ , 19____.

_____L.S.

The foregoing instrument was signed by _____ as his/her Last Will and Testament in our presence and we in his/her presence and in each other's presence have signed the same as witnesses thereto.

_____residing at_____

_____residing at_____

Last Will and Testament

I, _____ a resident of _____ , Massachusetts do hereby make, publish and declare this to be my Last Will and Testament, hereby revoking any and all Wills and Codicils heretofore made by me.

FIRST: I direct that all my just debts and funeral expenses be paid out of my estate as soon after my death as is practicable.

SECOND: I may leave a statement or list disposing of certain items of my tangible personal property. Any such statement or list in existence at the time of my death shall be determinative with respect to all items bequeathed therein.

THIRD: All the rest, residue and remainder of my estate, real or personal, wheresoever situate, now owned or hereafter acquired by me, which at the time of my death shall belong to me or be subject to my disposal by Will, I give devise and bequeath unto my spouse, _____.

FOURTH: In the event that my said spouse predeceases me, or fails to survive me by thirty days, then I give devise and bequeath the rest, residue and remainder of my estate unto my children, _____ _____.

FIFTH: I hereby nominate, constitute and appoint _____ as guardian over the person of any of my children who have not reached the age of majority at the time of my death. In the event that said guardian is unable or unwilling to serve then I nominate, constitute and appoint _____ as guardian.

SIXTH: I hereby nominate, constitute and appoint _____ as guardian over the estate of any of my children who have not reached the age of majority at the time of my death. In the event that said guardian is unable or unwilling to serve then I nominate, constitute and appoint _____ as guardian.

SEVENTH: I hereby nominate, constitute and appoint _____ to serve as Executor (Executrix) of this, my Last Will and Testament, to serve without bond or surety. In the event that he or she is unable or unwilling to serve at any time for any reason then I nominate, constitute and appoint _____ as alternate Executor (Executrix) also to serve without bond or surety. I give my said Executor (Executrix) the fullest power in all matters including the power to sell or convey real or personal property or any interest therein without court order.

IN WITNESS WHEREOF I have signed and published this my Last Will and Testament this _____ day of _____, 19____.

_____L.S.

The foregoing instrument was signed by _____ as his/her Last Will and Testament in our presence and we in his/her presence and in each other's presence have signed the same as witnesses thereto.

_____residing at_____

_____residing at_____

Last Will and Testament

I, _____ a resident of _____ , Massachusetts do hereby make, publish and declare this to be my Last Will and Testament, hereby revoking any and all Wills and Codicils heretofore made by me.

FIRST: I direct that all my just debts and funeral expenses be paid out of my estate as soon after my death as is practicable.

SECOND: I may leave a statement or list disposing of certain items of my tangible personal property. Any such statement or list in existence at the time of my death shall be determinative with respect to all items bequeathed therein.

THIRD: All the rest, residue and remainder of my estate, real or personal, wheresoever situate, now owned or hereafter acquired by me, which at the time of my death shall belong to me or be subject to my disposal by Will, I give devise and bequeath unto my spouse, _____ .

FOURTH: In the event that my said spouse predeceases me, or fails to survive me by thirty days, then I give devise and bequeath the rest, residue and remainder of my estate unto my children, _____ _____ .

FIFTH: I hereby nominate, constitute and appoint _____ as guardian over the person of any of my children who have not reached the age of majority at the time of my death. In the event that said guardian is unable or unwilling to serve then I nominate, constitute and appoint _____ as guardian.

SIXTH: I hereby nominate, constitute and appoint _____ as guardian over the estate of any of my children who have not reached the age of majority at the time of my death. In the event that said guardian is unable or unwilling to serve then I nominate, constitute and appoint _____ as guardian.

SEVENTH: I hereby nominate, constitute and appoint _____ to serve as Executor (Executrix) of this, my Last Will and Testament, to serve without bond or surety. In the event that he or she is unable or unwilling to serve at any time for any reason then I nominate, constitute and appoint _____ as alternate Executor (Executrix) also to serve without bond or surety. I give my said Executor (Executrix) the fullest power in all matters including the power to sell or convey real or personal property or any interest therein without court order.

IN WITNESS WHEREOF I have signed and published this my Last Will and Testament this _____ day of _____, 19____ .

_____L.S.

The foregoing instrument was signed by _____ as his/her Last Will and Testament in our presence and we in his/her presence and in each other's presence have signed the same as witnesses thereto.

_____residing at_____

_____residing at_____

Last Will and Testament

I, _____ a resident of _____ , Massachusetts do hereby make, publish and declare this to be my Last Will and Testament, hereby revoking any and all Wills and Codicils heretofore made by me.

FIRST: I direct that all my just debts and funeral expenses be paid out of my estate as soon after my death as is practicable.

SECOND: I may leave a statement or list disposing of certain items of my tangible personal property. Any such statement or list in existence at the time of my death shall be determinative with respect to all items bequeathed therein.

THIRD: All the rest, residue and remainder of my estate, real or personal, wheresoever situate, now owned or hereafter acquired by me, which at the time of my death shall belong to me or be subject to my disposal by Will, I give devise and bequeath unto my spouse, _____.

FOURTH: In the event that my said spouse predeceases me, or fails to survive me by thirty days, then I give devise and bequeath the rest, residue and remainder of my estate unto my children, _____.

FIFTH: In the event that any of my children have not reached the age of ____ years at the time of my death, then the share of any such child shall be held IN TRUST by _____ until such time as such child or children reach the age of ____ years. The trustee shall use the income and that part of the principal of the trust as is, in the discretion of the trustee, necessary or desirable to provide proper housing, medical care, food, clothing, entertainment and education for the trust beneficiaries. In the event the said trustee is unable or unwilling to serve for any reason, then I nominate, constitute and appoint _____ as alternate trustee. No bond shall be required of either trustee.

SIXTH: I hereby nominate, constitute and appoint _____ as guardian over the person of any of my children who have not reached the age of majority at the time of my death. In the event that said guardian is unable or unwilling to serve then I nominate, constitute and appoint _____ as guardian.

SEVENTH: I hereby nominate, constitute and appoint _____ to serve as Executor (Executrix) of this, my Last Will and Testament, to serve without bond or surety. In the event that he or she is unable or unwilling to serve at any time for any reason then I nominate, constitute and appoint _____ as alternate Executor (Executrix) also to serve without bond or surety. I give my said Executor (Executrix) the fullest power in all matters including the power to sell or convey real or personal property or any interest therein without court order.

IN WITNESS WHEREOF I have signed and published this my Last Will and Testament this _____ day of _____, 19____.

_____L.S.

The foregoing instrument was signed by _____ as his/her Last Will and Testament in our presence and we in his/her presence and in each other's presence have signed the same as witnesses thereto.

_____residing at_____

_____residing at_____

Last Will and Testament

I, _____ a resident of _____ , Massachusetts do hereby make, publish and declare this to be my Last Will and Testament, hereby revoking any and all Wills and Codicils heretofore made by me.

FIRST: I direct that all my just debts and funeral expenses be paid out of my estate as soon after my death as is practicable.

SECOND: I may leave a statement or list disposing of certain items of my tangible personal property. Any such statement or list in existence at the time of my death shall be determinative with respect to all items bequeathed therein.

THIRD: All the rest, residue and remainder of my estate, real or personal, wheresoever situate, now owned or hereafter acquired by me, which at the time of my death shall belong to me or be subject to my disposal by Will, I give devise and bequeath unto my spouse, _____.

FOURTH: In the event that my said spouse predeceases me, or fails to survive me by thirty days, then I give devise and bequeath the rest, residue and remainder of my estate unto my children, _____.

FIFTH: In the event that any of my children have not reached the age of ____ years at the time of my death, then the share of any such child shall be held IN TRUST by _____ until such time as such child or children reach the age of ____ years. The trustee shall use the income and that part of the principal of the trust as is, in the discretion of the trustee, necessary or desirable to provide proper housing, medical care, food, clothing, entertainment and education for the trust beneficiaries. In the event the said trustee is unable or unwilling to serve for any reason, then I nominate, constitute and appoint _____ as alternate trustee. No bond shall be required of either trustee.

SIXTH: I hereby nominate, constitute and appoint _____ as guardian over the person of any of my children who have not reached the age of majority at the time of my death. In the event that said guardian is unable or unwilling to serve then I nominate, constitute and appoint _____ as guardian.

SEVENTH: I hereby nominate, constitute and appoint _____ to serve as Executor (Executrix) of this, my Last Will and Testament, to serve without bond or surety. In the event that he or she is unable or unwilling to serve at any time for any reason then I nominate, constitute and appoint _____ as alternate Executor (Executrix) also to serve without bond or surety. I give my said Executor (Executrix) the fullest power in all matters including the power to sell or convey real or personal property or any interest therein without court order.

IN WITNESS WHEREOF I have signed and published this my Last Will and Testament this _____ day of _____, 19____.

_____L.S.

The foregoing instrument was signed by _____ as his/her Last Will and Testament in our presence and we in his/her presence and in each other's presence have signed the same as witnesses thereto.

_____residing at_____

_____residing at_____

Last Will and Testament

I, _____ a resident of _____ , Massachusetts do hereby make, publish and declare this to be my Last Will and Testament, hereby revoking any and all Wills and Codicils heretofore made by me.

FIRST: I direct that all my just debts and funeral expenses be paid out of my estate as soon after my death as is practicable.

SECOND: I may leave a statement or list disposing of certain items of my tangible personal property. Any such statement or list in existence at the time of my death shall be determinative with respect to all items bequeathed therein.

THIRD: All the rest, residue and remainder of my estate, real or personal, wheresoever situate, now owned or hereafter acquired by me, which at the time of my death shall belong to me or be subject to my disposal by Will, I give devise and bequeath unto the following persons or to the survivors of them:

_____% to my spouse_____;

_____% in equal shares to my children: _____

_____

FOURTH: If any person named in this Will shall fail to survive me by thirty days then this Will shall take effect as if that person had predeceased me.

FIFTH: I hereby nominate, constitute and appoint _____ _____ to serve as Executor (Executrix) of this, my Last Will and Testament, to serve without bond or surety. In the event that he or she is unable or unwilling to serve at any time for any reason then I nominate, constitute and appoint _____ as alternate Executor (Executrix) also to serve without bond or surety. I give my said Executor (Executrix) the fullest power in all matters including the power to sell or convey real or personal property or any interest therein without court order.

IN WITNESS WHEREOF I have signed and published this my Last Will and Testament this _____ day of _____, 19____.

_____L.S.

The foregoing instrument was signed by _____ as his/her Last Will and Testament in our presence and we in his/her presence and in each other's presence have signed the same as witnesses thereto.

_____residing at_____

_____residing at_____

Last Will and Testament

I, _____ a resident of _____ , Massachusetts do hereby make, publish and declare this to be my Last Will and Testament, hereby revoking any and all Wills and Codicils heretofore made by me.

FIRST: I direct that all my just debts and funeral expenses be paid out of my estate as soon after my death as is practicable.

SECOND: I may leave a statement or list disposing of certain items of my tangible personal property. Any such statement or list in existence at the time of my death shall be determinative with respect to all items bequeathed therein.

THIRD: All the rest, residue and remainder of my estate, real or personal, wheresoever situate, now owned or hereafter acquired by me, which at the time of my death shall belong to me or be subject to my disposal by Will, I give devise and bequeath unto the following persons or to the survivors of them:

_____% to my spouse_____;
_____% in equal shares to my children: _____

_____

FOURTH: If any person named in this Will shall fail to survive me by thirty days then this Will shall take effect as if that person had predeceased me.

FIFTH: I hereby nominate, constitute and appoint _____ _____ to serve as Executor (Executrix) of this, my Last Will and Testament, to serve without bond or surety. In the event that he or she is unable or unwilling to serve at any time for any reason then I nominate, constitute and appoint _____ as alternate Executor (Executrix) also to serve without bond or surety. I give my said Executor (Executrix) the fullest power in all matters including the power to sell or convey real or personal property or any interest therein without court order.

IN WITNESS WHEREOF I have signed and published this my Last Will and Testament this _____ day of _____, 19____.

_____L.S.

The foregoing instrument was signed by _____ as his/her Last Will and Testament in our presence and we in his/her presence and in each other's presence have signed the same as witnesses thereto.

_____residing at_____

_____residing at_____

Last Will and Testament

I, _____ a resident of _____ , Massachusetts do hereby make, publish and declare this to be my Last Will and Testament, hereby revoking any and all Wills and Codicils heretofore made by me.

FIRST: I direct that all my just debts and funeral expenses be paid out of my estate as soon after my death as is practicable.

SECOND: I may leave a statement or list disposing of certain items of my tangible personal property. Any such statement or list in existence at the time of my death shall be determinative with respect to all items bequeathed therein.

THIRD: All the rest, residue and remainder of my estate, real or personal, wheresoever situate, now owned or hereafter acquired by me, which at the time of my death shall belong to me or be subject to my disposal by Will, I give devise and bequeath unto the following persons or to the survivors of them:

_____% to my spouse_____;
_____% to _____;
_____% to _____;
_____% to _____;
_____% to _____.

FOURTH: If any person named in this Will shall fail to survive me by thirty days then this Will shall take effect as if that person had predeceased me.

FIFTH: I hereby nominate, constitute and appoint_____ _____ to serve as Executor (Executrix) of this, my Last Will and Testament, to serve without bond or surety. In the event that he or she is unable or unwilling to serve at any time for any reason then I nominate, constitute and appoint _____ as alternate Executor (Executrix) also to serve without bond or surety. I give my said Executor (Executrix) the fullest power in all matters including the power to sell or convey real or personal property or any interest therein without court order.

IN WITNESS WHEREOF I have signed and published this my Last Will and Testament this _____ day of _____, 19____.

_____L.S.

The foregoing instrument was signed by _____ as his/her Last Will and Testament in our presence and we in his/her presence and in each other's presence have signed the same as witnesses thereto.

_____residing at_____

_____residing at_____

Last Will and Testament

I, _____ a resident of _____ , Massachusetts do hereby make, publish and declare this to be my Last Will and Testament, hereby revoking any and all Wills and Codicils heretofore made by me.

FIRST: I direct that all my just debts and funeral expenses be paid out of my estate as soon after my death as is practicable.

SECOND: I may leave a statement or list disposing of certain items of my tangible personal property. Any such statement or list in existence at the time of my death shall be determinative with respect to all items bequeathed therein.

THIRD: All the rest, residue and remainder of my estate, real or personal, wheresoever situate, now owned or hereafter acquired by me, which at the time of my death shall belong to me or be subject to my disposal by Will, I give devise and bequeath unto the following persons or to the survivors of them:

_____% to my spouse_____ ;
_____% to _____ ;
_____% to _____ ;
_____% to _____ ;
_____% to _____ .

FOURTH: If any person named in this Will shall fail to survive me by thirty days then this Will shall take effect as if that person had predeceased me.

FIFTH: I hereby nominate, constitute and appoint_____ _____ to serve as Executor (Executrix) of this, my Last Will and Testament, to serve without bond or surety. In the event that he or she is unable or unwilling to serve at any time for any reason then I nominate, constitute and appoint _____ as alternate Executor (Executrix) also to serve without bond or surety. I give my said Executor (Executrix) the fullest power in all matters including the power to sell or convey real or personal property or any interest therein without court order.

IN WITNESS WHEREOF I have signed and published this my Last Will and Testament this _____ day of _____ , 19____.

_____L.S.

The foregoing instrument was signed by _____ as his/her Last Will and Testament in our presence and we in his/her presence and in each other's presence have signed the same as witnesses thereto.

_____residing at_____

_____residing at_____

Last Will and Testament

I, _____ a resident of _____ , Massachusetts do hereby make, publish and declare this to be my Last Will and Testament, hereby revoking any and all Wills and Codicils heretofore made by me.

FIRST: I direct that all my just debts and funeral expenses be paid out of my estate as soon after my death as is practicable.

SECOND: I may leave a statement or list disposing of certain items of my tangible personal property. Any such statement or list in existence at the time of my death shall be determinative with respect to all items bequeathed therein.

THIRD: All the rest, residue and remainder of my estate, real or personal, wheresoever situate, now owned or hereafter acquired by me, which at the time of my death shall belong to me or be subject to my disposal by Will, I give devise and bequeath in equal shares to my children, _____ _____ _____.

FOURTH: If any person named in this Will shall fail to survive me by thirty days then this Will shall take effect as if that person had predeceased me.

FIFTH: I hereby nominate, constitute and appoint _____ as guardian over the person and estate of any of my children who have not reached the age of majority at the time of my death. In the event that said guardian is unable or unwilling to serve then I nominate, constitute and appoint _____ as guardian.

SIXTH: I hereby nominate, constitute and appoint _____ to serve as Executor (Executrix) of this, my Last Will and Testament, to serve without bond or surety. In the event that he or she is unable or unwilling to serve at any time for any reason then I nominate, constitute and appoint _____ as alternate Executor (Executrix) also to serve without bond or surety. I give my said Executor (Executrix) the fullest power in all matters including the power to sell or convey real or personal property or any interest therein without court order.

IN WITNESS WHEREOF I have signed and published this my Last Will and Testament this _____ day of _____ , 19____.

_____L.S.

The foregoing instrument was signed by _____ as his/her Last Will and Testament in our presence and we in his/her presence and in each other's presence have signed the same as witnesses thereto.

_____residing at_____

_____residing at_____

Last Will and Testament

I, _____ a resident of _____ , Massachusetts do hereby make, publish and declare this to be my Last Will and Testament, hereby revoking any and all Wills and Codicils heretofore made by me.

FIRST: I direct that all my just debts and funeral expenses be paid out of my estate as soon after my death as is practicable.

SECOND: I may leave a statement or list disposing of certain items of my tangible personal property. Any such statement or list in existence at the time of my death shall be determinative with respect to all items bequeathed therein.

THIRD: All the rest, residue and remainder of my estate, real or personal, wheresoever situate, now owned or hereafter acquired by me, which at the time of my death shall belong to me or be subject to my disposal by Will, I give devise and bequeath in equal shares to my children, _____ _____ _____.

FOURTH: If any person named in this Will shall fail to survive me by thirty days then this Will shall take effect as if that person had predeceased me.

FIFTH: I hereby nominate, constitute and appoint _____ as guardian over the person and estate of any of my children who have not reached the age of majority at the time of my death. In the event that said guardian is unable or unwilling to serve then I nominate, constitute and appoint _____ as guardian.

SIXTH: I hereby nominate, constitute and appoint _____ to serve as Executor (Executrix) of this, my Last Will and Testament, to serve without bond or surety. In the event that he or she is unable or unwilling to serve at any time for any reason then I nominate, constitute and appoint _____ as alternate Executor (Executrix) also to serve without bond or surety. I give my said Executor (Executrix) the fullest power in all matters including the power to sell or convey real or personal property or any interest therein without court order.

IN WITNESS WHEREOF I have signed and published this my Last Will and Testament this _____ day of _____, 19____.

_____L.S.

The foregoing instrument was signed by _____ as his/her Last Will and Testament in our presence and we in his/her presence and in each other's presence have signed the same as witnesses thereto.

_____residing at_____

_____residing at_____

Last Will and Testament

I, _____ a resident of _____ , Massachusetts do hereby make, publish and declare this to be my Last Will and Testament, hereby revoking any and all Wills and Codicils heretofore made by me.

FIRST: I direct that all my just debts and funeral expenses be paid out of my estate as soon after my death as is practicable.

SECOND: I may leave a statement or list disposing of certain items of my tangible personal property. Any such statement or list in existence at the time of my death shall be determinative with respect to all items bequeathed therein.

THIRD: All the rest, residue and remainder of my estate, real or personal, wheresoever situate, now owned or hereafter acquired by me, which at the time of my death shall belong to me or be subject to my disposal by Will, I give devise and bequeath in equal shares to my children, _____ _____.

FOURTH: If any person named in this Will shall fail to survive me by thirty days then this Will shall take effect as if that person had predeceased me.

FIFTH: I hereby nominate, constitute and appoint _____ as guardian over the person of any of my children who have not reached the age of majority at the time of my death. In the event that said guardian is unable or unwilling to serve then I nominate, constitute and appoint _____ as guardian.

SIXTH: I hereby nominate, constitute and appoint _____ as guardian over the estate of any of my children who have not reached the age of majority at the time of my death. In the event that said guardian is unable or unwilling to serve then I nominate, constitute and appoint _____ as guardian.

SEVENTH: I hereby nominate, constitute and appoint _____ to serve as Executor (Executrix) of this, my Last Will and Testament, to serve without bond or surety. In the event that he or she is unable or unwilling to serve at any time for any reason then I nominate, constitute and appoint _____ as alternate Executor (Executrix) also to serve without bond or surety. I give my said Executor (Executrix) the fullest power in all matters including the power to sell or convey real or personal property or any interest therein without court order.

IN WITNESS WHEREOF I have signed and published this my Last Will and Testament this _____ day of _____, 19____.

_____L.S.

The foregoing instrument was signed by _____ as his/her Last Will and Testament in our presence and we in his/her presence and in each other's presence have signed the same as witnesses thereto.

_____residing at_____

_____residing at_____

Last Will and Testament

I, _____ a resident of _____ , Massachusetts do hereby make, publish and declare this to be my Last Will and Testament, hereby revoking any and all Wills and Codicils heretofore made by me.

FIRST: I direct that all my just debts and funeral expenses be paid out of my estate as soon after my death as is practicable.

SECOND: I may leave a statement or list disposing of certain items of my tangible personal property. Any such statement or list in existence at the time of my death shall be determinative with respect to all items bequeathed therein.

THIRD: All the rest, residue and remainder of my estate, real or personal, wheresoever situate, now owned or hereafter acquired by me, which at the time of my death shall belong to me or be subject to my disposal by Will, I give devise and bequeath in equal shares to my children, _____ _____.

FOURTH: If any person named in this Will shall fail to survive me by thirty days then this Will shall take effect as if that person had predeceased me.

FIFTH: I hereby nominate, constitute and appoint _____ as guardian over the person of any of my children who have not reached the age of majority at the time of my death. In the event that said guardian is unable or unwilling to serve then I nominate, constitute and appoint _____ as guardian.

SIXTH: I hereby nominate, constitute and appoint _____ as guardian over the estate of any of my children who have not reached the age of majority at the time of my death. In the event that said guardian is unable or unwilling to serve then I nominate, constitute and appoint _____ as guardian.

SEVENTH: I hereby nominate, constitute and appoint _____ to serve as Executor (Executrix) of this, my Last Will and Testament, to serve without bond or surety. In the event that he or she is unable or unwilling to serve at any time for any reason then I nominate, constitute and appoint _____ as alternate Executor (Executrix) also to serve without bond or surety. I give my said Executor (Executrix) the fullest power in all matters including the power to sell or convey real or personal property or any interest therein without court order.

IN WITNESS WHEREOF I have signed and published this my Last Will and Testament this _____ day of _____, 19____.

_____L.S.

The foregoing instrument was signed by _____ as his/her Last Will and Testament in our presence and we in his/her presence and in each other's presence have signed the same as witnesses thereto.

_____residing at_____

_____residing at_____

Last Will and Testament

I, _____ a resident of _____ , Massachusetts do hereby make, publish and declare this to be my Last Will and Testament, hereby revoking any and all Wills and Codicils heretofore made by me.

FIRST: I direct that all my just debts and funeral expenses be paid out of my estate as soon after my death as is practicable.

SECOND: I may leave a statement or list disposing of certain items of my tangible personal property. Any such statement or list in existence at the time of my death shall be determinative with respect to all items bequeathed therein.

THIRD: All the rest, residue and remainder of my estate, real or personal, wheresoever situate, now owned or hereafter acquired by me, which at the time of my death shall belong to me or be subject to my disposal by Will, I give devise and bequeath in equal shares to my children, _____ _____.

FOURTH: If any person named in this Will shall fail to survive me by thirty days then this Will shall take effect as if that person had predeceased me.

FIFTH: In the event that any beneficiary has not reached the age of ____ years at the time of my death, then the share of any such beneficiary shall be held IN TRUST by _____ until such time as such beneficiary reaches the age of ____ years. The trustee shall use the income and that part of the principal of the trust as is in the discretion of the trustee necessary or desirable to provide proper housing, medical care, food, clothing, entertainment and education for the trust beneficiaries. In the event the said trustee is unable or unwilling to serve for any reason, then I nominate, constitute and appoint _____ as alternate trustee. No bond shall be required of either trustee. In the event any beneficiary does not reach said age, then his or her share shall pass to his or her lineal descendants or, if none, to the surviving residuary beneficiaries under this will.

SIXTH: I hereby nominate, constitute and appoint _____ as guardian over the person of any of my children who have not reached the age of majority at the time of my death. In the event that said guardian is unable or unwilling to serve then I nominate, constitute and appoint _____ as guardian.

SEVENTH: I hereby nominate, constitute and appoint _____ to serve as Executor (Executrix) of this, my Last Will and Testament, to serve without bond or surety. In the event that he or she is unable or unwilling to serve at any time for any reason then I nominate, constitute and appoint _____ as alternate Executor (Executrix) also to serve without bond or surety. I give my said Executor (Executrix) the fullest power in all matters including the power to sell or convey real or personal property or any interest therein without court order.

IN WITNESS WHEREOF I have signed and published this my Last Will and Testament this ____ day of _____ , 19____ .

_____L.S.

The foregoing instrument was signed by _____ as his/her Last Will and Testament in our presence and we in his/her presence and in each other's presence have signed the same as witnesses thereto.

_____residing at_____

_____residing at_____

Last Will and Testament

I, _____ a resident of _____ , Massachusetts do hereby make, publish and declare this to be my Last Will and Testament, hereby revoking any and all Wills and Codicils heretofore made by me.

FIRST: I direct that all my just debts and funeral expenses be paid out of my estate as soon after my death as is practicable.

SECOND: I may leave a statement or list disposing of certain items of my tangible personal property. Any such statement or list in existence at the time of my death shall be determinative with respect to all items bequeathed therein.

THIRD: All the rest, residue and remainder of my estate, real or personal, wheresoever situate, now owned or hereafter acquired by me, which at the time of my death shall belong to me or be subject to my disposal by Will, I give devise and bequeath in equal shares to my children, _____ _____.

FOURTH: If any person named in this Will shall fail to survive me by thirty days then this Will shall take effect as if that person had predeceased me.

FIFTH: In the event that any beneficiary has not reached the age of ____ years at the time of my death, then the share of any such beneficiary shall be held IN TRUST by _____ until such time as such beneficiary reaches the age of ____ years. The trustee shall use the income and that part of the principal of the trust as is in the discretion of the trustee necessary or desirable to provide proper housing, medical care, food, clothing, entertainment and education for the trust beneficiaries. In the event the said trustee is unable or unwilling to serve for any reason, then I nominate, constitute and appoint _____ as alternate trustee. No bond shall be required of either trustee. In the event any beneficiary does not reach said age, then his or her share shall pass to his or her lineal descendants or, if none, to the surviving residuary beneficiaries under this will.

SIXTH: I hereby nominate, constitute and appoint _____ as guardian over the person of any of my children who have not reached the age of majority at the time of my death. In the event that said guardian is unable or unwilling to serve then I nominate, constitute and appoint _____ as guardian.

SEVENTH: I hereby nominate, constitute and appoint _____ to serve as Executor (Executrix) of this, my Last Will and Testament, to serve without bond or surety. In the event that he or she is unable or unwilling to serve at any time for any reason then I nominate, constitute and appoint _____ as alternate Executor (Executrix) also to serve without bond or surety. I give my said Executor (Executrix) the fullest power in all matters including the power to sell or convey real or personal property or any interest therein without court order.

IN WITNESS WHEREOF I have signed and published this my Last Will and Testament this _____ day of _____, 19____.

_____L.S.

The foregoing instrument was signed by _____ as his/her Last Will and Testament in our presence and we in his/her presence and in each other's presence have signed the same as witnesses thereto.

_____residing at_____

_____residing at_____

Last Will and Testament

I, _____ a resident of _____ , Massachusetts do hereby make, publish and declare this to be my Last Will and Testament, hereby revoking any and all Wills and Codicils heretofore made by me.

FIRST: I direct that all my just debts and funeral expenses be paid out of my estate as soon after my death as is practicable.

SECOND: I may leave a statement or list disposing of certain items of my tangible personal property. Any such statement or list in existence at the time of my death shall be determinative with respect to all items bequeathed therein.

THIRD: All the rest, residue and remainder of my estate, real or personal, wheresoever situate, now owned or hereafter acquired by me, which at the time of my death shall belong to me or be subject to my disposal by Will, I give devise and bequeath unto the following persons or to the survivors of them:

_____% to _____;
_____% to _____;
_____% to _____;
_____% to _____;
_____% to _____.

FOURTH: If any person named in this Will shall fail to survive me by thirty days then this Will shall take effect as if that person had predeceased me.

FIFTH: I hereby nominate, constitute and appoint _____ _____ to serve as Executor (Executrix) of this, my Last Will and Testament, to serve without bond or surety. In the event that he or she is unable or unwilling to serve at any time for any reason then I nominate, constitute and appoint _____ as alternate Executor (Executrix) also to serve without bond or surety. I give my said Executor (Executrix) the fullest power in all matters including the power to sell or convey real or personal property or any interest therein without court order.

IN WITNESS WHEREOF I have signed and published this my Last Will and Testament this _____ day of _____, 19____.

_____L.S.

The foregoing instrument was signed by _____ as his/her Last Will and Testament in our presence and we in his/her presence and in each other's presence have signed the same as witnesses thereto.

_____residing at_____

_____residing at_____

Last Will and Testament

I, _____ a resident of _____ , Massachusetts do hereby make, publish and declare this to be my Last Will and Testament, hereby revoking any and all Wills and Codicils heretofore made by me.

FIRST: I direct that all my just debts and funeral expenses be paid out of my estate as soon after my death as is practicable.

SECOND: I may leave a statement or list disposing of certain items of my tangible personal property. Any such statement or list in existence at the time of my death shall be determinative with respect to all items bequeathed therein.

THIRD: All the rest, residue and remainder of my estate, real or personal, wheresoever situate, now owned or hereafter acquired by me, which at the time of my death shall belong to me or be subject to my disposal by Will, I give devise and bequeath unto the following persons or to the survivors of them:

_____% to _____ ;
_____% to _____ ;
_____% to _____ ;
_____% to _____ ;
_____% to _____ .

FOURTH: If any person named in this Will shall fail to survive me by thirty days then this Will shall take effect as if that person had predeceased me.

FIFTH: I hereby nominate, constitute and appoint _____ _____ to serve as Executor (Executrix) of this, my Last Will and Testament, to serve without bond or surety. In the event that he or she is unable or unwilling to serve at any time for any reason then I nominate, constitute and appoint _____ as alternate Executor (Executrix) also to serve without bond or surety. I give my said Executor (Executrix) the fullest power in all matters including the power to sell or convey real or personal property or any interest therein without court order.

IN WITNESS WHEREOF I have signed and published this my Last Will and Testament this _____ day of _____, 19____.

_____L.S.

The foregoing instrument was signed by _____ as his/her Last Will and Testament in our presence and we in his/her presence and in each other's presence have signed the same as witnesses thereto.

_____residing at_____

_____residing at_____

SELF-PROVED WILL PAGE
(attach to Will)

COMMONWEALTH OF MASSACHUSETTS

COUNTY OF _____

We, _____, _____, and
_____ the testator and the witnesses respectively,
whose names are signed to the attached or foregoing instrument, having been
sworn, declared to the undersigned officer that the testator, in the presence of
witnesses, signed the instrument as his/her last will, that he/she signed, and
that each of the witnesses, in the presence of the testator and in the presence of
each other, signed the will as witnesses.

_____
Testator_____

_____
Witness_____

_____
Witness_____

Subscribed and sworn to before me by _____ the
testator, and by _____ and _____,
the witnesses, all of whom personally appeared before me on _____,
19____. The testator, _____ is personally known
to me or has produced _____ as identification,
_____ is personally known to me or has produced
_____ as identification _____
is personally known to me or has produced _____
as identification.

_____
Notary Public
My commission expires:

(Notary Seal)

SELF-PROVED WILL PAGE
(attach to Will)

COMMONWEALTH OF MASSACHUSETTS

COUNTY OF _____

We, _____, _____, and
_____ the testator and the witnesses respectively,
whose names are signed to the attached or foregoing instrument, having been
sworn, declared to the undersigned officer that the testator, in the presence of
witnesses, signed the instrument as his/her last will, that he/she signed, and
that each of the witnesses, in the presence of the testator and in the presence of
each other, signed the will as witnesses.

_____

Testator_____

_____

Witness_____

_____

Witness_____

Subscribed and sworn to before me by _____ the
testator, and by _____ and _____,
the witnesses, all of whom personally appeared before me on _____,
19____. The testator, _____ is personally known
to me or has produced _____ as identification,
_____ is personally known to me or has produced
_____ as identification _____
is personally known to me or has produced _____
as identification.

_____

Notary Public
My commission expires:

(Notary Seal)

First Codicil to the Will of

_____

I, _____, a resident of _____,
Massachusetts declare this to be the first codicil to my Last Will and Testament dated
_____, 19____.

FIRST: I hereby revoke the clause of my Will which reads as follows: _____
_____
_____
_____

SECOND: I hereby add following clause to my Will: _____
_____
_____
_____
_____

THIRD: In all other respects I hereby confirm and republish my Last Will and Testament
dated _____, 19____.

Date: _____   _____L.S.

The foregoing instrument was signed by _____ as his/her
First Codicil to Will in our presence and we in his/her presence and in the presence of each other
have signed the same as witnesses thereto.

_____residing at _____

_____residing at _____

COMMONWEALTH OF MASSACHUSETTS
COUNTY OF _____

We, _____, _____, and
_____ the testator and the witnesses respectively, whose names are
signed to the attached or foregoing instrument, having been sworn, declared to the undersigned
officer that the testator, in the presence of witnesses, signed the instrument as his/her last will,
that he/she signed, and that each of the witnesses, in the presence of the testator and in the
presence of each other, signed the will as witnesses.

_____   _____
Testator   Witness

                                        _____
                                        Witness

Subscribed and sworn to before me by _____ the testator, and
by _____ and _____, the witnesses, all of whom
personally appeared before me on _____, 19____. The testator,
_____ is personally known to me or has produced
_____ as identification, _____
is personally known to me or has produced _____ as
identification _____ is personally known to me or has produced
_____ as identification.

                                        _____
                                        Notary Public
(Notary Seal)   My commission expires:

79

First Codicil to the Will of

_____

I, _____, a resident of _____,
Massachusetts declare this to be the first codicil to my Last Will and Testament dated
_____, 19____.

      FIRST: I hereby revoke the clause of my Will which reads as follows: _____
_____
_____
_____

      SECOND: I hereby add following clause to my Will: _____
_____
_____
_____
_____

      THIRD: In all other respects I hereby confirm and republish my Last Will and Testament
dated _____, 19____.

Date: _____   _____L.S.

      The foregoing instrument was signed by _____ as his/her
First Codicil to Will in our presence and we in his/her presence and in the presence of each other
have signed the same as witnesses thereto.

_____residing at _____

_____residing at _____

COMMONWEALTH OF MASSACHUSETTS
COUNTY OF _____
      We, _____, _____, and
_____ the testator and the witnesses respectively, whose names are
signed to the attached or foregoing instrument, having been sworn, declared to the undersigned
officer that the testator, in the presence of witnesses, signed the instrument as his/her last will,
that he/she signed, and that each of the witnesses, in the presence of the testator and in the
presence of each other, signed the will as witnesses.

_____   _____

Testator   Witness

                                             _____

                                             Witness

      Subscribed and sworn to before me by _____ the testator, and
by _____ and _____, the witnesses, all of whom
personally appeared before me on _____, 19____. The testator,
_____ is personally known to me or has produced
_____ as identification, _____
is personally known to me or has produced _____ as
identification _____ is personally known to me or has produced
_____ as identification.

                                             _____
                                             Notary Public
(Notary Seal)   My commission expires:

Living Will and Health Care Proxy
of

_____

ARTICLE I: LIVING WILL

KNOW ALL MEN BY THESE PRESENTS: That I, _____ of _____ , Commonwealth of Massachusetts, do hereby make, publish and declare ARTICLE I of this instrument to be my Living Will. This Living Will shall have no effect upon, and shall not revoke or cancel, any other wills, codicils or testamentary dispositions heretofore made by me. This Living Will shall also have no effect on the validity of my Health Care Proxy contained in Article II of this Instrument.

A. If my death cannot be avoided, and if I have lost the ability to interact with others and have no reasonable chance of regaining this ability, or if my suffering is intense and irreversible, I wish to have the following expressions of my desire respected and acted upon by the individuals mentioned hereinbelow:

1. I do not want to have my life prolonged.

2. I would not wish to have life support from mechanical devices or other life prolonging procedures.

Notwithstanding the foregoing, I would want to have care that gives comfort and support and that facilitates my interaction with others to the extent that is possible and which brings peace.

B. I do not fear death itself as much as the indignities of deterioration, dependence and hopeless pain. I therefore ask that medication be mercifully administered to me to alleviate suffering, even though so doing may hasten the moment of death.

ARTICLE II: HEALTH CARE PROXY

<u>KNOW ALL MEN BY THESE PRESENTS:</u> That I, _____, (hereinafter also the "Principal"), a legal resident of _____, Commonwealth of Massachusetts, do hereby make, publish and declare ARTICLE II of this instrument to be my HEALTH CARE PROXY and by these presents in ARTICLE II do make, constitute and appoint _____ of _____, Massachusetts my true and lawful health care agent (hereinafter the "Agent") and do hereby grant said Agent authority to make health care decisions on my behalf, said authority taking effort upon a determination, pursuant to the provisions of ARTICLE II Sections (A) and (B) below, that I lack the capacity to make or to communicate such health care decisions. It is my intention herein to appoint a health care agent and to create a valid and binding HEALTH CARE PROXY pursuant to Massachusetts General Laws ch. 201D and to comply with the provisions thereunder.

A. The determination that I lack the capacity to make or to communicate health care decisions shall be made in writing by the attending physician according to accepted standards of medical judgment and shall contain said attending physician's opinion regarding the cause and nature of my incapacity as well as the extent and probable duration of such incapacity.

B. If the attending physician determines that I have the capacity to make or to communicate health care decisions: 1) the authority of the Agent shall cease; and 2) my consent for treatment shall be required.

C. The Agent shall have the authority, pursuant to the provisions of this HEALTH CARE PROXY, to make any and all health care decisions on my behalf including decisions about life sustaining treatment after an independent doctor concurs with my physician that there is no chance of my recovery. The Agent may look to my Living Will in Article I of this instrument for guidance in making such health care decisions provided that the Agent's sole interpretation of my Living Will shall be binding and conclusive on all persons.

D. I request that health care providers comply with the Agent's health care decisions to the same extent as if I had made such decisions.

E. No health care provider or employee thereof shall be subject to criminal or civil liability or be deemed to have engaged in unprofessional conduct, for carrying out in good faith the Agent's health care decisions pursuant to this HEALTH CARE PROXY.

F. No person acting as Agent pursuant to this HEALTH CARE PROXY shall be subject to criminal or civil liability for making a health care decision pursuant to this HEALTH CARE PROXY.

G. In the event that my Agent, _____, shall be unavailable or shall for any reason, including removal, death, incapacity or resignation, cease to serve or fail to qualify as Agent hereunder, then I designate _____ to serve as alternate Agent with full power and authority thereunder.

H. In the event that any one or more of the provisions contained in this instrument shall for any reason be held to be invalid, illegal, or unenforceable in any respect, such validity, illegality or unenforceability shall not affect the validity, legality, or enforceability of any of the other provisions of this instrument.

IN WITNESS WHEREOF, I, _____, do hereto set my hand and in the presence of the Witnesses publish and declare this Instrument, typewritten on this page and the other preceding numbered sheets, one side only being used, and each preceding page having been initialed by me, to be my LIVING WILL and HEALTH CARE PROXY this _____ day of _____ , 199___.

_____,
Principal

Signed, sealed, published and declared by _____, as for, and acknowledged by _____ to be his Living Will and Health Care Proxy, in the presence of the undersigned, who at his request, in his presence and in the presence of each other, have hereunto subscribed our names as Witnesses the day and year first written above and hereby affirm that each of us is at least eighteen (18) years of age and that the principal appeared to be at least eighteen (18) years of age, of sound mind and under no constraint or undue influence.

_____   of   _____
                                                                                  _____

_____   of   _____
                                                                                  _____

COMMONWEALTH OF MASSACHUSETTS

_____ , SS   Date:

Then personally appeared the above _____, and acknowledged the foregoing instrument to be his free act and deed before me,

_____
Notary Public
My Commission Expires:

Living Will and Health Care Proxy
of

_____

ARTICLE I: LIVING WILL

KNOW ALL MEN BY THESE PRESENTS: That I, _____ of _____ , Commonwealth of Massachusetts, do hereby make, publish and declare ARTICLE I of this instrument to be my Living Will. This Living Will shall have no effect upon, and shall not revoke or cancel, any other wills, codicils or testamentary dispositions heretofore made by me. This Living Will shall also have no effect on the validity of my Health Care Proxy contained in Article II of this Instrument.

A. If my death cannot be avoided, and if I have lost the ability to interact with others and have no reasonable chance of regaining this ability, or if my suffering is intense and irreversible, I wish to have the following expressions of my desire respected and acted upon by the individuals mentioned hereinbelow:

1. I do not want to have my life prolonged.

2. I would not wish to have life support from mechanical devices or other life prolonging procedures.

Notwithstanding the foregoing, I would want to have care that gives comfort and support and that facilitates my interaction with others to the extent that is possible and which brings peace.

B. I do not fear death itself as much as the indignities of deterioration, dependence and hopeless pain. I therefore ask that medication be mercifully administered to me to alleviate suffering, even though so doing may hasten the moment of death.

ARTICLE II: HEALTH CARE PROXY

KNOW ALL MEN BY THESE PRESENTS: That I, _____ , (hereinafter also the "Principal"), a legal resident of _____, Commonwealth of Massachusetts, do hereby make, publish and declare ARTICLE II of this instrument to be my HEALTH CARE PROXY and by these presents in ARTICLE II do make, constitute and appoint _____ of _____ , Massachusetts my true and lawful health care agent (hereinafter the "Agent") and do hereby grant said Agent authority to make health care decisions on my behalf, said authority taking effort upon a determination, pursuant to the provisions of ARTICLE II Sections (A) and (B) below, that I lack the capacity to make or to communicate such health care decisions. It is my intention herein to appoint a health care agent and to create a valid and binding HEALTH CARE PROXY pursuant to Massachusetts General Laws ch. 201D and to comply with the provisions thereunder.

A. The determination that I lack the capacity to make or to communicate health care decisions shall be made in writing by the attending physician according to accepted standards of medical judgment and shall contain said attending physician's opinion regarding the cause and nature of my incapacity as well as the extent and probable duration of such incapacity.

B. If the attending physician determines that I have the capacity to make or to communicate health care decisions: 1) the authority of the Agent shall cease; and 2) my consent for treatment shall be required.

C. The Agent shall have the authority, pursuant to the provisions of this HEALTH CARE PROXY, to make any and all health care decisions on my behalf including decisions about life sustaining treatment after an independent doctor concurs with my physician that there is no chance of my recovery. The Agent may look to my Living Will in Article I of this instrument for guidance in making such health care decisions provided that the Agent's sole interpretation of my Living Will shall be binding and conclusive on all persons.

D. I request that health care providers comply with the Agent's health care decisions to the same extent as if I had made such decisions.

E. No health care provider or employee thereof shall be subject to criminal or civil liability or be deemed to have engaged in unprofessional conduct, for carrying out in good faith the Agent's health care decisions pursuant to this HEALTH CARE PROXY.

F. No person acting as Agent pursuant to this HEALTH CARE PROXY shall be subject to criminal or civil liability for making a health care decision pursuant to this HEALTH CARE PROXY.

G. In the event that my Agent, _____, shall be unavailable or shall for any reason, including removal, death, incapacity or resignation, cease to serve or fail to qualify as Agent hereunder, then I designate _____ to serve as alternate Agent with full power and authority thereunder.

H. In the event that any one or more of the provisions contained in this instrument shall for any reason be held to be invalid, illegal, or unenforceable in any respect, such validity, illegality or unenforceability shall not affect the validity, legality, or enforceability of any of the other provisions of this instrument.

IN WITNESS WHEREOF, I, _____, do hereto set my hand and in the presence of the Witnesses publish and declare this Instrument, typewritten on this page and the other preceding numbered sheets, one side only being used, and each preceding page having been initialed by me, to be my LIVING WILL and HEALTH CARE PROXY this _____ day of _____ , 199___.

_____,
Principal

Signed, sealed, published and declared by _____, as for, and acknowledged by _____ to be his Living Will and Health Care Proxy, in the presence of the undersigned, who at his request, in his presence and in the presence of each other, have hereunto subscribed our names as Witnesses the day and year first written above and hereby affirm that each of us is at least eighteen (18) years of age and that the principal appeared to be at least eighteen (18) years of age, of sound mind and under no constraint or undue influence.

_____   of   _____
_____

_____   of   _____
_____

COMMONWEALTH OF MASSACHUSETTS

_____, SS   **Date:**

Then personally appeared the above _____, and acknowledged the foregoing instrument to be his free act and deed before me,

_____
Notary Public
My Commission Expires:

UNIFORM DONOR CARD

The undersigned hereby makes this anatomical gift, if medically acceptable, to take effect on death.   The words and marks below indicate my desires:

I give:

      (a) ____ any needed organs or parts;

      (b) ____ only the following organs or parts

_____

for the purpose of transplantation, therapy, medical research, or education;

      (c) ____ my body for anatomical study if needed.

Limitations or special wishes, if any:

_____

Signed by the donor and the following witnesses in the presence of each other:

_____   _____
Signature of Donor   Date of birth

_____   _____
Date signed   City & State

_____   _____
Witness   Witness

_____   _____
Address   Address

UNIFORM DONOR CARD

The undersigned hereby makes this anatomical gift, if medically acceptable, to take effect on death.   The words and marks below indicate my desires:

I give:

      (a) ____ any needed organs or parts;

      (b) ____ only the following organs or parts

_____

for the purpose of transplantation, therapy, medical research, or education;

      (c) ____ my body for anatomical study if needed.

Limitations or special wishes, if any:

_____

Signed by the donor and the following witnesses in the presence of each other:

_____   _____
Signature of Donor   Date of birth

_____   _____
Date signed   City & State

_____   _____
Witness   Witness

_____   _____
Address   Address

UNIFORM DONOR CARD

The undersigned hereby makes this anatomical gift, if medically acceptable, to take effect on death.   The words and marks below indicate my desires:

I give:

      (a) ____ any needed organs or parts;

      (b) ____ only the following organs or parts

_____

for the purpose of transplantation, therapy, medical research, or education;

      (c) ____ my body for anatomical study if needed.

Limitations or special wishes, if any:

_____

Signed by the donor and the following witnesses in the presence of each other:

_____   _____
Signature of Donor   Date of birth

_____   _____
Date signed   City & State

_____   _____
Witness   Witness

_____   _____
Address   Address

UNIFORM DONOR CARD

The undersigned hereby makes this anatomical gift, if medically acceptable, to take effect on death.   The words and marks below indicate my desires:

I give:

      (a) ____ any needed organs or parts;

      (b) ____ only the following organs or parts

_____

for the purpose of transplantation, therapy, medical research, or education;

      (c) ____ my body for anatomical study if needed.

Limitations or special wishes, if any:

_____

Signed by the donor and the following witnesses in the presence of each other:

_____   _____
Signature of Donor   Date of birth

_____   _____
Date signed   City & State

_____   _____
Witness   Witness

_____   _____
Address   Address

These cards should be cut out and carried in your wallet or purse.

A.   Simple Will - Property to Spouse or Adult Children

Last Will and Testament

I, _____John Smith_____ a resident of _North Reading_ ,Massachusetts do hereby make, publish and declare this to be my Last Will and Testament, hereby revoking any and all Wills and Codicils heretofore made by me.

FIRST: I direct that all my just debts and funeral expenses be paid out of my estate as soon after my death as is practicable.

SECOND: I may leave a statement or list disposing of certain items of my tangible personal property. Any such statement or list in existence at the time of my death shall be determinative with respect to all items bequeathed therein.

THIRD: All the rest, residue and remainder of my estate, real or personal, wheresoever situate, now owned or hereafter acquired by me, which at the time of my death shall belong to me or be subject to my disposal by Will, I give devise and bequeath unto my spouse, _____Barbara Smith_____ .

FOURTH: In the event that my said spouse predeceases me, or fails to survive me by thirty days, then I give devise and bequeath the rest, residue and remainder of my estate unto my children, _Amy Smith, Beamy Smith and Seamy Smith_ _in equal shares_ .

FIFTH: I hereby nominate, constitute and appoint __Barbara Smith__ to serve as ~~Executor~~ (Executrix) of this, my Last Will and Testament, to serve without bond or surety. In the event that he or she is unable or unwilling to serve at any time or for any reason then I nominate, constitute and appoint _____Reginald_____ _Smith_ as alternate Executor (~~Executrix~~) also to serve without bond or surety. I give my said Executor (Executrix) the fullest power in all matters including the power to sell or convey real or personal property or any interest therein without court order.

IN WITNESS WHEREOF I have signed and published this my Last Will and Testament this _5th_ day of _January_ , 19_97_ .

John Smith L.S.

The foregoing Instrument was signed by _____John Smith_____ as his/her Last Will and Testament in our presence and we in his/her presence and in each other's presence have signed the same as witnesses thereto.

Brenda Jones residing at _Boston, Massachusetts_

James Earl Jones residing at _Wakefield, Mass._

Last Will and Testament

I, _____Woody Allen_____ a resident of _____Revere_____ , Massachusetts do hereby make, publish and declare this to be my Last Will and Testament, hereby revoking any and all Wills and Codicils heretofore made by me.

FIRST: I direct that all my just debts and funeral expenses be paid out of my estate as soon after my death as is practicable.

SECOND: I may leave a statement or list disposing of certain items of my tangible personal property. Any such statement or list in existence at the time of my death shall be determinative with respect to all items bequeathed therein.

THIRD: All the rest, residue and remainder of my estate, real or personal, wheresoever situate, now owned or hereafter acquired by me, which at the time of my death shall belong to me or be subject to my disposal by Will, I give devise and bequeath unto the following persons or to the survivors of them:

      _50_ % to my spouse _Soon Yi Previn Allen_ ;
      _20_ % to _____Mia Farrow_____ ;
      _20_ % to _____Diane Keaton_____ ;
      _10_ % to _____Louise Lasser_____ ;
      _____ % to _____ .

FOURTH: If any person named in this Will shall fail to survive me by thirty days then this Will shall take effect as if that person had predeceased me.

FIFTH: I hereby nominate, constitute and appoint_Soon Yi Previn Allen_ to serve as ~~Executor~~ (Executrix) of this, my Last Will and Testament, to serve without bond or surety. In the event that he or she is unable or unwilling to serve at any time for any reason then I nominate, constitute and appoint _____Mia Farrow_____ as alternate ~~Executor~~ (Executrix) also to serve without bond or surety. I give my said ~~Executor~~ (Executrix) the fullest power in all matters including the power to sell or convey real or personal property or any interest therein without court order.

IN WITNESS WHEREOF I have signed and published this my Last Will and Testament this _29_ day of _January_ , 19 _97_ .

                                    *Woody Allen*_____ L.S.

The foregoing instrument was signed by _____Woody Allen_____ as his/her Last Will and Testament in our presence and we in his/her presence and in each other's presence have signed the same as witnesses thereto.

_Annie Hall_____ residing at_Andover, MA_

_Fielding Mellish_____ residing at_Worcester, Mass._

Last Will and Testament

I, _____John Doe_____ a resident of _____Pittsfield_____, Massachusetts do hereby make, publish and declare this to be my Last Will and Testament, hereby revoking any and all Wills and Codicils heretofore made by me.

FIRST: I direct that all my just debts and funeral expenses be paid out of my estate as soon after my death as is practicable.

SECOND: I may leave a statement or list disposing of certain items of my tangible personal property. Any such statement or list in existence at the time of my death shall be determinative with respect to all items bequeathed therein.

THIRD: All the rest, residue and remainder of my estate, real or personal, wheresoever situate, now owned or hereafter acquired by me, which at the time of my death shall belong to me or be subject to my disposal by Will, I give devise and bequeath in equal shares to my children, _____James Doe, Mary Doe, Larry Doe, Barry Doe, Carrie Doe and Moe Doe_____ _____.

FOURTH: If any person named in this Will shall fail to survive me by thirty days then this Will shall take effect as if that person had predeceased me.

FIFTH: I hereby nominate, constitute and appoint _____Herbert Doe_____ as guardian over the person of any of my children who have not reached the age of majority at the time of my death. In the event that said guardian is unable or unwilling to serve then I nominate, constitute and appoint _____Tom Doe_____ as guardian.

SIXTH: I hereby nominate, constitute and appoint _____Clarence Doe_____ as guardian over the estate of any of my children who have not reached the age of majority at the time of my death. In the event that said guardian is unable or unwilling to serve then I nominate, constitute and appoint _____Englebert Doe_____ as guardian.

SEVENTH: I hereby nominate, constitute and appoint _____Clarence Doe_____ to serve as Executor (Executrix) of this, my Last Will and Testament, to serve without bond or surety. In the event that he or she is unable or unwilling to serve at any time for any reason then I nominate, constitute and appoint _____Englebert Doe_____ as alternate Executor (Executrix) also to serve without bond or surety. I give my said Executor (Executrix) the fullest power in all matters including the power to sell or convey real or personal property or any interest therein without court order.

IN WITNESS WHEREOF I have signed and published this my Last Will and Testament this _2nd_ day of _July_, 19_97_.

_____ L.S.

The foregoing instrument was signed by _____John Doe_____ as his/her Last Will and Testament in our presence and we in his/her presence and in each other's presence have signed the same as witnesses thereto.

_____Jane Roe_____ residing at _Framingham, MA_

_____Melvin Coe_____ residing at _New Bedford, MA_

SELF-PROVED WILL PAGE
(attach to Will)

COMMONWEALTH OF MASSACHUSETTS

COUNTY OF ___Essex___

We, ___Larry Lowe___, ___Mary Hartman___, and ___Phyllis Diller___ the testator and the witnesses respectively, whose names are signed to the attached or foregoing instrument, having been sworn, declared to the undersigned officer that the testator, in the presence of witnesses, signed the instrument as his/her last will, that he/she signed, and that each of the witnesses, in the presence of the testator and in the presence of each other, signed the will as witnesses.

Testator___Larry Lowe___

Witness___Mary Hartman___

Witness___Phyllis Diller___

Subscribed and sworn to before me by ___Larry Lowe___ the testator, and by ___Mary Hartman___ and ___Phyllis Diller___, the witnesses, all of whom personally appeared before me on ___July 5,___, 19_97_. The testator,___Larry Lowe___ is personally known to me or has produced __MA. Dr. Lic #L123456__ as identification, ___Mary Hartman___ is personally known to me or has produced _MA. Dr. Lic #H987654321_ as identification ___Phyllis Diller___ is personally known to me or has produced ___MA Lic. #32___ as identification.

___John Galt___
Notary Public
My commission expires: 9/16/97

(Notary Seal)

First Codicil to the Will of

_____Larry Lowe_____

I, _____Larry Lowe_____, a resident of _____Lawrence_____, Massachusetts declare this to be the first codicil to my Last Will and Testament dated _____January 5_____, 19 _97_.

    FIRST: I hereby revoke the clause of my Will which reads as follows: _____
_____FOURTH: I hereby leave $5000.00 to my daughter Mildred_____

    SECOND: I hereby add following clause to my Will: _____
_____FOURTH: I hereby leave $1000.00 to my daughter Mildred_____

    THIRD: In all other respects I hereby confirm and republish my Last Will and Testament dated _____January 5_____, 19 _96_.

Date: _____July 5, 1997_____   _Larry Lowe_ L.S.

    The foregoing instrument was signed by _____Larry Lowe_____ as his/her First Codicil to Will in our presence and we in his/her presence and in the presence of each other have signed the same as witnesses thereto.

Mary Hartman residing at _Fitchburg, Mass._

Phyllis Diller residing at _Quincy, Massachusetts_

COMMONWEALTH OF MASSACHUSETTS
COUNTY OF _____Essex_____

    We, _____Larry Lowe_____, _____Mary Hartman_____, and _____Phyllis Diller_____ the testator and the witnesses respectively, whose names are signed to the attached or foregoing instrument, having been sworn, declared to the undersigned officer that the testator, in the presence of witnesses, signed the instrument as his/her last will, that he/she signed, and that each of the witnesses, in the presence of the testator and in the presence of each other, signed the will as witnesses.

Larry Lowe
Testator

Mary Hartman
Witness

Phyllis Diller
Witness

    Subscribed and sworn to before me by _____Larry Lowe_____ the testator, and by _____Mary Hartman_____ and _____Phyllis Diller_, the witnesses, all of whom personally appeared before me on _____July 5,_____, 19 _97_. The testator, _____Larry Lowe_____ is personally known to me or has produced _____MA. Dr. Lic #L123456_____ as identification, _____Mary Hartman_____ is personally known to me or has produced _____MA. Dr. Lic #H987654321_____ as identification _____Phyllis Diller_____ is personally known to me or has produced _____MA. Lic. #32_____ as identification.

John Holt
Notary Public
My commission expires: _9/16/97_

(Notary Seal)

Living Will and Health Care Proxy
of

John Smith

ARTICLE I: LIVING WILL

KNOW ALL MEN BY THESE PRESENTS: That I, _____ John Smith _____ of
_____ Springfield _____ , Commonwealth of Massachusetts, do hereby make, publish and declare ARTICLE I of this instrument to be my Living Will. This Living Will shall have no effect upon, and shall not revoke or cancel, any other wills, codicils or testamentary dispositions heretofore made by me. This Living Will shall also have no effect on the validity of my Health Care Proxy contained in Article II of this Instrument.

A. If my death cannot be avoided, and if I have lost the ability to interact with others and have no reasonable chance of regaining this ability, or if my suffering is intense and irreversible, I wish to have the following expressions of my desire respected and acted upon by the individuals mentioned hereinbelow:

1. I do not want to have my life prolonged.

2. I would not wish to have life support from mechanical devices or other life prolonging procedures.

Notwithstanding the foregoing, I would want to have care that gives comfort and support and that facilitates my interaction with others to the extent that is possible and which brings peace.

B. I do not fear death itself as much as the indignities of deterioration, dependence and hopeless pain. I therefore ask that medication be mercifully administered to me to alleviate suffering, even though so doing may hasten the moment of death.

ARTICLE II: HEALTH CARE PROXY

KNOW ALL MEN BY THESE PRESENTS: That I, _____ John Smith _____ , (hereinafter also the "Principal"), a legal resident of _____ Springfield _____ , Commonwealth of Massachusetts, do hereby make, publish and declare ARTICLE II of this instrument to be my HEALTH CARE PROXY and by these presents in ARTICLE II do make, constitute and appoint _____ Mary Smith of Springfield _____ , Massachusetts my true and lawful health care agent (hereinafter the "Agent") and do hereby grant said Agent authority to make health care decisions on my behalf, said authority taking effort upon a determination, pursuant to the provisions of ARTICLE II Sections (A) and (B) below, that I lack the capacity to make or to communicate such health care decisions. It is my intention herein to appoint a health care agent and to create a valid and binding HEALTH CARE PROXY pursuant to Massachusetts General Laws ch. 201D and to comply with the provisions thereunder.

A. The determination that I lack the capacity to make or to communicate health care decisions shall be made in writing by the attending physician according to accepted standards of medical judgment and shall contain said attending physician's opinion regarding the cause and nature of my incapacity as well as the extent and probable duration of such incapacity.

B. If the attending physician determines that I have the capacity to make or to communicate health care decisions: 1) the authority of the Agent shall cease; and 2) my consent for treatment shall be required.

C. The Agent shall have the authority, pursuant to the provisions of this HEALTH CARE PROXY, to make any and all health care decisions on my behalf including decisions about life sustaining treatment after an independent doctor concurs with my physician that there is no chance of my recovery. The Agent may look to my Living Will in Article I of this instrument for guidance in making such health care decisions provided that the Agent's sole interpretation of my Living Will shall be binding and conclusive on all persons.

D. I request that health care providers comply with the Agent's health care decisions to the same extent as if I had made such decisions.

E. No health care provider or employee thereof shall be subject to criminal or civil liability or be deemed to have engaged in unprofessional conduct, for carrying out in good faith the Agent's health care decisions pursuant to this HEALTH CARE PROXY.

F. No person acting as Agent pursuant to this HEALTH CARE PROXY shall be subject to criminal or civil liability for making a health care decision pursuant to this HEALTH CARE PROXY.

G. In the event that my Agent, _____ Mary Smith _____, shall be unavailable or shall for any reason, including removal, death, incapacity or resignation, cease to serve or fail to qualify as Agent hereunder, then I designate ____ Margaret Jones ____ to serve as alternate Agent with full power and authority thereunder.

H. In the event that any one or more of the provisions contained in this instrument shall for any reason be held to be invalid, illegal, or unenforceable in any respect, such validity, illegality or unenforceability shall not affect the validity, legality, or enforceability of any of the other provisions of this instrument.

IN WITNESS WHEREOF, I, _____ John Smith _____, do hereto set my hand and in the presence of the Witnesses publish and declare this Instrument, typewritten on this page and the other preceding numbered sheets, one side only being used, and each preceding page having been initialed by me, to be my LIVING WILL and HEALTH CARE PROXY this _31st_ day of ____ August ____, 199_7_.

John Smith
Principal

Signed, sealed, published and declared by _____ John Smith _____, as for, and acknowledged by _____ John Smith _____ to be his Living Will and Health Care Proxy, in the presence of the undersigned, who at his request, in his presence and in the presence of each other, have hereunto subscribed our names as Witnesses the day and year first written above and hereby affirm that each of us is at least eighteen (18) years of age and that the principal appeared to be at least eighteen (18) years of age, of sound mind and under no constraint or undue influence.

Joseph Johnson   of   123 Main Street
Marie Johnson   Falmouth, Massachusetts

                          of   123 Main Street
                                     Falmouth, Massachusetts

COMMONWEALTH OF MASSACHUSETTS

Middlesex , **SS**   **Date:** 8/31/97

Then personally appeared the above _____ John Smith _____, and acknowledged the foregoing instrument to be his free act and deed before me,

Christopher R. Offering
Notary Public
My Commission Expires: 2/2/01

INDEX

Alternate beneficiaries, 20
Anatomical gifts, 31

Bonds, 11
Bond, Surety, 15

Changing will, 28
Children, 12
Codicil, 28
Copy of will, 26
Commissioner, 17

Divorce, 13
Donor card, 31, 87

Elective share, 9
Execution of will, 25
Executor, 15, 23

Forced share, 9
Forms, 24, 33-87
Funeral arrangements, 24

Guardian, 15, 22

Health care proxy, 29

Illegal provisions, 17
Inheritance taxes, 18
I/T/F bank accounts, 11

Joint ownership, 8, 11
Joint tenancy, 8, 10

Living will, 29, 83

Marriage, 12

Out-of-state wills, 17

Pay on death accounts, 11
Per capita, 21
Per stirpes, 21
Personal property, 19
Probate, 7, 8

Remainder clause, 20
Revoking will, 27

Securities, 11
Self-proved will, 17, 23, 26, 28, 75, 77
Signing will, 24
Specific bequests, 20
Spousal rights, 9
Stocks, 11
Storage of will, 27
Survivorship, 22

Tenants in common, 8
Totten trusts, 11
Trusts, 7, 16

Uniform donor card, 31, 87
Unreasonable conditions, 17
Using self-help law books, 6

Witnesses, 23, 25

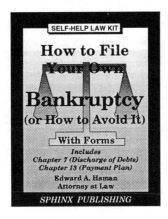
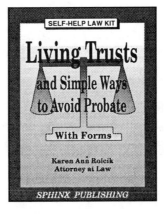

National Title	ISBN Number	Price
Crime Victims' Guide to Justice	1-57248-048-3	19.95
Debtors' Rights, A Legal Self-Help Guide, 2nd ed.	1-57248-023-8	12.95
Defend Yourself Against **Criminal Charges**	1-57248-059-9	19.95
Divorces From Hell	1-57248-017-3	10.95
Grandparents' Rights	1-57248-001-7	19.95
Guia de Inmigración a Estados Unidos (Spanish ed. Immigration Guide)	0-913825-99-9	19.95
Help Your Lawyer Win Your Case	1-57248-021-1	12.95
How to **Buy a Condominium or Townhome**	1-57248-061-0	16.95
How to File Your Own **Bankruptcy**, 3rd Ed.	0-913825-98-0	19.95
How to Form Your Own **Corporation**	0-913825-61-1	19.95
How to Negotiate **Real Estate Contracts**, 2nd Ed.	1-57248-035-1	16.95
How to Negotiate **Real Estate Leases**, 2nd Ed.	1-57248-036-X	16.95
How to Register Your Own **Copyright**	1-57248-002-5	19.95
How to Register Your Own **Trademark**	0-913825-88-3	19.95
How to Write Your Own **Living Will**	1-57248-060-2	9.95
How to Write Your Own **Premarital Agreement**	0-913825-69-7	19.95
Jurors' Rights	1-57248-031-9	9.95
Lawsuits of the Rich & Famous	0-913825-95-6	10.95
Legal Malpractice and Other Claims Against Your Lawyer	1-57248-032-7	18.95
Legal Research Made Easy	1-57248-008-4	14.95
Living Trusts & Simple Ways to Avoid Probate	1-57248-019X	19.95
The Most Valuable **Business Forms** You'll Ever Need	1-57248-022-X	19.95
The Most Valuable **Corporate Forms** You'll Ever Need	1-57248-007-6	24.95
Neighbor vs. Neighbor: Legal Rights of Neighbors in Dispute	0-913825-41-7	12.95
The **Power of Attorney** Handbook, 2nd Ed.	1-57248-044-0	19.95
Simple Ways to **Protect Yourself From Lawsuits**	1-57248-020-3	24.95
Social Security Benefits Handbook	1-57248-033-5	14.95
Software Law: A User Friendly Legal Guide for Software Developer's	1-57248-049-1	24.95
Successful **Real Estate Brokerage Management**	0-913825-86-7	19.95
U.S.A. **Immigration** Guide, 2nd Ed.	1-57248-000-9	19.95
Victims' Rights: The Complete Guide to Crime Victim Compensation	0-913825-82-4	12.95
Winning Your **Personal Injury** Claim	1-57248-052-1	19.95

Self-Help Law for Massachusetts !

•Written by Massachusetts Attorneys•
•Forms & Instructions Included•

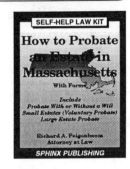

Provides all of the information and forms needed to file for divorce in Massachusetts, without the expense of hiring a lawyer. Includes property division, alimony, and child support, custody & visitation.

Without a will, Masschusetts probate laws decide who gets your property. This book explains the law regarding wills and joint property, inheritance laws and living wills. Includes 14 forms with instructions.

Includes what you need to know about licensing, sales tax, name registration, labor laws, unemployment taxes, regulatory laws, worker compensation, advertising rules, and labor laws. Also includes forms.

Covering all aspects of the law, from property inspections and occupancy permits to tenant applications, and from security deposits to evictions, this book is invaluable for any residental or commercial landlord.

Save precious capital by forming your own corporation without the expense of a lawyer. Includes an explanation of corporation law, start-up procedures, tax considerations, and forms with instructions.

Save hundreds, or even thousands, of dollars in legal fees with our do-it-yourself legal guides.

Title	ISBN Number	Price
How to File for Divorce in Massachusetts	1-57248-051-4	19.95
How to Make a Massachusetts Will	1-57248-050-5	9.95
How to Probate an Estate in Massachusetts	1-57248-053-X	19.95
How to Start a Business in Massachusetts	1-57248-054-8	16.95
Landlords' Rights & Duties in Massachusetts	1-57248-055-6	19.95

[Don't miss our national self-help law kits on the next page!]

Also available, self-help law books for:
Alabama, Florida, Georgia, Illinois, Michigan, Minnesota,
North Carolina, South Carolina, and Texas
Call for information: 1-800-226-5291

- -